The Tanks of World War II: The History and Legacy of Tank Warfare between the Allies and Axis

By Charles River Editors

German tanks in 1942

About Charles River Editors

Charles River Editors provides superior editing and original writing services across the digital publishing industry, with the expertise to create digital content for publishers across a vast range of subject matter. In addition to providing original digital content for third party publishers, we also republish civilization's greatest literary works, bringing them to new generations of readers via ebooks.

Sign up here to receive updates about free books as we publish them, and visit Our Kindle Author Page to browse today's free promotions and our most recently published Kindle titles.

About the Author

Sean McLachlan is a military historian and archaeologist who has explored World War I battlefields in Belgium, Bulgaria, Turkey, Italy, and Iraq. He has written numerous books and articles on military history and is also the author of several works of fiction, including the *Trench Raiders* series of World War I action novels. For more information, check out his Amazon page and blog.

Introduction

A German Tiger I tank

The Tanks of World War II

"In this year, 1929, I became convinced that tanks working on their own or in conjunction with infantry could never achieve decisive importance. My historical studies, the exercises carried out in England and our own experience with mock-ups had persuaded me that the tanks would never be able to produce their full effect until the other weapons on whose support they must inevitably rely were brought up to their standard of speed and of cross-country performance. In such formation of all arms, the tanks must play primary role, the other weapons beings subordinated to the requirements of the armour. It would be wrong to include tanks in infantry divisions; what was needed were armoured divisions which would include all the supporting arms needed to allow the tanks to fight with full effect." – Heinz Guderian

War has always been a competition between defense and offense. At times these two have been relatively balanced, but at other times, one becomes far more powerful. It is during those times that the greatest military innovations occur.

The tank was first developed by the British and French during World War I as a means to break the deadlock on the Western Front. More so than any previous war, the balance of power lay with the defense, as machine guns, trenches, bunkers, barbed wire, and rapid-firing rifles all made frontal assaults on established positions prohibitively costly. In the closing months of the war, the tank partially evened up that balance, even as the war's commanders initially proved unsure of how to use them. While it cannot be said that the tank won the war, it contributed to its end and if the fighting had continued another year, the mass production that had started in Allied countries may have proved decisive.

All major powers, and many minor ones, learned their lesson in World War I. During the interwar period (late 1918 to mid-1939), a wide variety of tanks and antitank weapons were developed by a number of different countries, and those nations that did not have their own models hastened to purchase some from the more advanced countries. These tanks would shape the war that was to come.

World War II was thus the culmination of a quarter century of tank development, and it would also be the first major test of tanks in mobile warfare, during which they had to face other tanks. However, many of the tanks were constructed with the static warfare of the Western Front in mind and were thus slow and had short operational ranges. Others were too light to face opposing tanks or the new generation of anti-tank weapons that hadn't existed in World War I. The unsuitability of these tank models for this new kind of warfare was quickly recognized, and the belligerent powers scrambled to create better designs. As each new, improved model came off the assembly lines, the opposing powers rushed to create a tank that could beat it. In that regard, World War II was also a war between rival engineers.

At the same time, German military officials were at the forefront of developing new ideologies when it came to utilizing their tanks to maximum effect. Heinz Guderian even published a book on the topic before becoming one of the Third Reich's most effective tank commanders. Moreover, during the German invasion of Poland, Nazi forces gained experience they would use across Europe and in Russia. After all, it was in Poland that the Wehrmacht saw action for the first time, conducting what was not only an invasion but also a trial run of its new equipment and tactics. The Polish invasion proved invaluable in providing the German high command with a low-risk, high-value live fire exercise for their newly minted war machine, while the actual combat experience highlighted the remaining flaws in the system. During the campaign, the Germans honed tactics and weapon systems for the massive struggle with the Soviets, British, and United States that loomed on the horizon.

The beginning of World War II found the major powers developing tanks to some extent, but lingering ideas from World War I affected the development of tanks during the Interwar period. As a result, aside from the blitzkrieg doctrine developed by the Nazis, tanks were still used in terms of infantry support, and there were few wars during this period to give strategists the chance to develop better uses for the new armored vehicles before World War II started. Commanders soon found that many of the tanks fielded in the campaigns of 1939-1941 lacked the necessary armor, guns, and designs.

One problem with the early models was that their armor was not steeply sloped, which was important because sloped armor helped deflect shells and gave a practical thickness greater than the actual thickness. It took some time for tank designers to appreciate this, and the leaders in this field were the Soviets and their T-34, arguably the best all-around tank of the war. Early German encounters with the T-34 during the opening phases of Operation Barbarossa in 1941 made them realize that sloping armor was vital, and their later models' armor, such as that of the Panzer V, had a steeper slope.

The Allies learned from the Germans as well. The first and most obvious lesson was to equip each tank with a radio. At the beginning of the war, most Allied tanks did not have radios and used small flags to signal to each other, an unreliable means under ideal conditions, let alone in the midst of battlefield chaos. The Panzers, on the other hand, were equipped with radios from the very start, providing German tank commanders with far more control over their units.

Throughout the war, designers learned how to improve suspension, reorganize the interior to give the crews more room, and incorporate other upgrades that helped with the overall function of the tank. Practical experience from the tank crews was of vital importance in these developments.

Inevitably, tactics evolved throughout the war. The Germans were early leaders in tank tactics, as their successes from Poland through the opening phases of Operation Barbarossa demonstrated. The main German tank tactic was the so-called *Schwerpunkt* ("center of gravity"), in which a concentration of tanks achieved a local superiority, broke through, and drove deep behind enemy lines, carving up frontline enemy forces that could then be surrounded and taken out by support tanks, infantry, and artillery. This is why German tanks were built for speed while maintaining good armor and weaponry.

In the early part of the war, Allied tanks spread out to act as infantry support, but once the Allies witnessed the efficacy of German tank tactics, they began to imitate them, prompting the Germans to further refine their own techniques.

The Tanks of World War II: The History and Legacy of Tank Warfare between the Allies and Axis looks at the development of the tanks and the doctrines that revolutionized tank warfare. Along with pictures of important people, places, and events, you will learn about the tanks of World War II like never before.

The Tanks of World War II: The History and Legacy of Tank Warfare between the Allies and Axis
About Charles River Editors
About the Author
Introduction
  Note
  The Development of Tanks after World War I
  Heinz Guderian and the Development of Tank Doctrine
  Blitzkrieg in Poland
  French Tanks
  The Conquest of Belgium and France
  The Early Stages of the North Africa Campaign
  The Eastern Front
  Allied Tanks in North Africa and Western Europe
  Later German Models
  Later Soviet Models
  Tanks in Other Theaters
  Anti-Tank Weapons
  The End of the War
  Conclusion
  Online Resources
  Bibliography
Free Books by Charles River Editors
Discounted Books by Charles River Editors

Note

Vehicle dimensions are given as length x width x height. To give consistency, both metric and Imperial units are given in fractions. The term "ton" refers to short tons, which is equal to 2,000 pounds (907.18474 kg), as opposed to long tons or metric tons. Maximum speed given is road speed. Speed over terrain could be much slower. Range is how far a tank could go without refueling. Once again this is based on road travel, with off-road travel range varying depending on the terrain. Armor thickness is maximum thickness. The thickest armor was generally found on the front and turret. Side armor was often thinner. Back and bottom armor almost always thinner in an effort to save material and weight.

The Development of Tanks after World War I

World War I ended with the Allies having a vast superiority in technical know-how when it came to tanks, but the Germans would learn from this mistake and remedy it in the 1930s as the Nazis rearmed the nation. Their first attempts were small, light tanks like the Panzer I and II, which aimed to replicate the success of the Renault FT, before moving on to heavier tanks such as the Panzer III. Moreover, men on both sides would use their experience and the time between wars to revolutionize tank warfare, including the likes of Erwin Rommel, Heinz Guderian, and George Patton.

While the tanks of World War I were superseded in the interwar period, the Renault FT was used to fight the Germans during the invasion of France in 1940. Perhaps not surprisingly, it proved to be outmatched by the Panzer IIs and Panzer IIIs it faced, showing that while it had been one of the most successful models of the Great War, it had been outpaced by the maneuverability and firepower of the German tanks in the 1940s.

Despite this, many of the old armored car designs continued to be produced and used throughout World War II for fighting infantry, especially against poorly armed partisans who did not have many antitank weapons. They also saw service in reconnaissance missions and as infantry support, as their speed and maneuverability were still useful on a more modern battlefield.

During the period between the two conflicts, the types of tanks mainly fell into two classes, reflecting the two main types of tanks in World War I. There were large, heavy tanks armed with one or more cannons and machine guns, and there were smaller, faster tanks (often called "tankettes") that had a light cannon or machine gun. The large tanks were lumbering beasts that moved at walking speed, but while they worked struck fear in the heart of the enemy, they proved vulnerable to field guns and were so slow as to be of little use outside the static conditions of the Western Front. Thanks to the successes of the light French Renault FT-17 during World War I, developers in the Interwar period generally favored the smaller, faster models of tanks.

George Patton standing in front of a Renault FT tank during World War I

The basic Renault FT model was armed with a single Hotchkiss 8mm (.31 in) Model 1914 machine gun. It had a crew of two (commandeer/gunner and driver), weighed 6.7 tons, and measured 5 m x 1.74 m x 2.14 m (16.4 x 5.7 x 7.02 ft). The hull had 16 mm (.63 in) armor on the front and 8 mm (.31 in) on the sides, while the turret had riveted 16 mm armor or a stronger cast turret of 22 mm (.87 in). It had a maximum speed of 7.5 km/h (4.8 mph) and a range of 35 km (25 mi). It could cross a trench 1.8 meters (6 ft) wide and a vertical obstacle .65 meters (2 ft) high. This last feature was especially important in trench warfare.

Two variants were introduced. The char canon replaced the machine gun with a 37 mm (1.46 in) gun and the char signal had a boxier, fixed turret to hold a wireless set. This latter model was deemed a failure by the men because the wireless set often broke down and the antennae were prone to damage. Using "bee swarm" tactics, the Renaults were able to overwhelm German positions in several offensives that saw the use of hundreds of these little tanks.

By the end of World War I, both the United Kingdom and France were mass producing tanks, and other nations such as the United States were also experimenting with armored vehicles. This development continued, but there were few chances to test the new weapons. This led to many odd designs that soon proved impractical once they were put to the test in an actual battlefield.

Several Interwar tank models had two turrets, both capable of firing straight forwards or backwards while each would take care of the flanks on their own. A few models even had three turrets, a main one in the center and two smaller ones on the front. These turrets all required more crewmembers, meaning the tanks had to be bigger. If they were bigger and were fitted with decent armor, then they were too heavy to move quickly. If speed was desired, then the armor had to be made too thin. Soon developers shifted designs to having only one turret with a main gun, usually but not always an artillery piece. Some tanks were only provided with machine guns.

Another experiment was having fixed guns on the front of the hull and not having a turret at all. This had obvious disadvantages, but some models persisted into the early years of World War II. The design gained new life with self-propelled guns, tank destroyers, and heavy assault guns. These were basically large artillery pieces placed on a tank chassis and protected with minimal armor. Some were even open on the top and rear. Because these do not fit the strict definition of a tank, we will be dealing with them only tangentially here.

Germany, forbidden by the Treaty of Versailles from developing tanks, had to test its tanks in secret. Ironically, it was the fact that this same treaty limited the German army to 100,000 men that prompted Hitler to shift the focus to a more mechanized armed force. Since he initially assumed Germany would not be able to win any future war with manpower, the Germans would have to win it with superior technology, and that technology would come in the form of the innovative Panzer series of tanks.

Early Panzers were designed to be light and fast like most tanks of the Interwar period. The Panzer I was more accurately a tankette, an undersized tracked vehicle with a turret but at a much smaller scale than what one normally associates with the word "tank." Tankettes were popular in the Interwar period. The Panzer I measured 4.02 m x 2.6 m x 1.72 m (13.2 x 6.8 x 5.6 ft) and weighed 5.4 tons. It had a speed of 50 km/h (23 mph) and a range of 200 km (120 mi). The crew of two consisted of a driver and the gunner/commander, who fired a pair of coaxial 7.92 mm (0.3 in) machine guns. Its armor was quite thin, only 13 mm (0.51 in) at the thickest, and in parts only 7 mm (0.28 in). Thus it was much faster with a far better range than the old Renault FT, but at the sacrifice of armor. Throughout the war, tank engineers were always trying to strike a balance between protection, speed, and firepower.

A Panzer I during World War II

Mass production started in 1934 after extensive trials. The tank went through several variations in its short history. The most popular model was the Ausf. A (*Ausführung* or "model") with about 800 being built and the Ausf. B, of which 675 were built between 1936 and 1938. The main improvement with the Ausf. B was a superior engine that required the chassis to be 40 cm (15.7 in) longer. It also had an improved gearbox and suspension. The weight of this model was 5.8 tons.

The slightly more robust Panzer II went into production in 1936. This had a 20 mm (0.79 in) auto-cannon plus a coaxial MG 34 7.92 mm (0.3 in) machine gun, thus having far better firepower than the Panzer I. The auto-cannon was based on a flak gun and had a high rate of fire (600 rpm, although the tank could only store a fraction of that number of rounds) that gave it good armor penetration. The tank looked like a bigger version of the Panzer I and measured 4.81 m x 2.22 m x 1.99 m (15.78 × 7.28 × 6.53 ft), weighed 8.9 tons, and had 5 mm (.2 in) to 15 mm (.59 in) of armor. Its maximum speed was 40 km/h (25 mph) with a range of 200 km (120 mi). It had a crew of three—a driver, loader/radio operator, and gunner/commander.

Despite the shortcomings of its thin armor, the Panzer II remained in use throughout the war, serving as a scout on the front and performing police duties in occupied territories long after heavier tanks ruled the front lines.

A Panzer II

Both the Panzer I and II were only seen as temporary models while medium tanks such as the Panzer III and IV were perfected. Production of the Panzer III was delayed during the Interwar period as German industry struggled to adapt to making tanks, and like other Panzers, the Panzer III went through many different variations. It was first armored with a 37 mm (1.46 in) gun. Many complained this was underpowered, but since it was the standard German infantry support gun, there were already many in store. Later versions upgraded to 50 mm (1.97 in) and finally a 75 mm (2.95 in) gun, greatly improving the Panzer III's ability to take on enemy tanks. General dimensions were 5.41 m x 2.95 m x 2.44 m (17.75 x 9.68 x 8.01 ft), with a speed of 40 km/h (25 mph) and a range of 165 km (102 mi). The crew of five (commander, gunner, loader, driver, radio operator/machine-gunner) manned the gun and two 7.92 mm (0.3 in) machine guns, one in the turret and the other in the front hull, an arrangement that became common for the tanks of many nations. While maximum armor in the early models was only 15 mm (0.59 in), later models were up-armored until the final models had up to 70 mm (2.76 in) of armor on the front. For much of its life, however, the Panzer III was under armored and undergunned considering what it had to face in the field. Nevertheless, nearly 6,000 were produced throughout the war and served in all theaters.

A Panzer III

The Panzer IV was even more powerful, but started production too late to serve in significant numbers in the early campaigns. Work on the very first prototype wasn't begun until 1936, and the first serviceable units rolled off the line that same year. Like other Panzers, it went through many variations. The Ausf. A to F1 used a short-barreled 75 mm (2.95 in) gun that proved insufficient against the heavier French and British tanks, so in preparation for the invasion of Russia the F2 to H models got a long 75 mm (2.95 in) gun capable of knocking out even the toughest Soviet armor. The tank measured .41 m x 2.88 m x 2.68 m (17.7 × 9.4 × 8.8 ft), weighed 25 tons, had armor ranging from 15 to 65 mm (0.59-2.56 in) thickness, had a speed of 42 km/h (26 mph), and a range of 200 km (120 mi). Its armaments were the above mentioned gun and two, or in some models three, 7.92 mm (0.3 in) machine guns. The roomy turret allowed for three men inside—the commander, gunner, and loader while the driver and radio operator/machine gunner sat in the front of the hull.

A Panzer IV during World War II

The Panzer IV would go on to become the Third Reich's most popular tank, with nearly 9,000 produced, but only 250 were available in September of 1939.

The nations not limited by the Treaty of Versailles proved less innovative than the Germans. Various colonial campaigns by France, Spain, and Italy in Africa witnessed little use of tanks, because generally the terrain was too rough to permit widespread use of tanks, and the native forces they faced were so outmatched in military technology as to not allow for a real test of the tanks' worth. Nevertheless, these colonial powers gained some insight into how to run tanks over long distances in dusty and hot conditions.

The real test of Interwar models came with the outbreak of the Spanish Civil War in 1936. The coalition Republican government, made up of various leftist parties including socialists and communists, faced an attempted coup by fascist Nationalist forces. Italy and later Germany sent tanks to aid the Nationalists while the Soviets sent tanks to help the Republicans. All three countries would gain valuable experience in the bitter three years of fighting, which consisted of battles in all types of terrain and conditions. In addition, many volunteers came from around the world to fight on one side or the other, thus becoming veterans before World War II even started.

This was also the first war to see tanks face anti-tank weapons. In World War I, these weapons had been in their infancy, so most tanks were knocked out with field artillery ill-suited for the task. In fact, more got bogged down in the mud and pocked terrain left by shells on the Western Front. Now, both the Republicans and Nationalists used anti-tank guns and various types of explosives to knock out tanks to some success. Once again, it appeared the balance of power shifted to the defense, although not nearly to such an extent as it had been in World War I.

In fact, tank developers had already anticipated such a problem. Anti-tank guns had seen some late use in World War I and developed rapidly thereafter. Thus, both the French and the British, and to a lesser extent other powers, shifted away from the lumbering behemoths of World War I to smaller, lighter tanks that could move in large numbers and outflank the enemy, wreaking havoc on rear areas and communication lines much like cavalry in the nineteenth century. While some tanks might be knocked out, their larger numbers would ensure success. This had already been tried to some extent in World War I with the French Renault FT-17.

During the Spanish Civil War, however, neither side had sufficient numbers of tanks to adopt such tactics. Also, commanders on both sides lacked the necessary experience to use their tanks properly. Tanks were generally used as infantry support or, even worse, sent out alone or in small numbers without any support in order to take limited objectives. This, of course, left them vulnerable to attack.

Of the various models deployed, the Italian Fiat L3/33 and L3/35 tankettes proved the worst. The latter model was the most numerous and slightly better armored than the former. Even so, the L3/35 measured only 3.17 m x 1.4 m x 1.3 m (10.4 × 4.59 × 4.27 ft), weighed 3.2 tons, with a speed of 42 km/h (26 mph) and a range of 125 km (78 mi). The driver and machine gunner were protected by a mere 6 to 12 mm (0.24-0.47 in) of armor that was vulnerable to concentrated machine gun fire. Armament consisted of twin-mounted 8 mm (0.31 in) machine guns located on the front of the hull rather than a turret. While the guns could swivel on a fairly wide arc, the lack of a turret made this model highly vulnerable to attacks to the flank and rear. Some later units were equipped with a front-mounted flamethrower.

These tankettes had shown their weakness even during the Ethiopian War, during which the Ethiopians had devised numerous techniques to pierce their thin armor. Some brave warriors even ran up behind the tankettes, making themselves safe from the front-mounted machine guns, and stuck their swords in the tracks, and the construction was so flimsy that this was often enough to disable the vehicle. Italian field commanders in both Ethiopia and Spain requested a heavier tank, but the cash-strapped army could not afford to develop one and continued production of the cheaper tankettes.

Despite these shortcomings, Mussolini's fascist government sent a total of 155 units to Spain during the Spanish Civil War, but the Germans provided more useful tanks in the form of three companies of Panzer Is (122 units).

The tanks performed well but were obviously outgunned by the Soviet T-26. On the Republican side, the armies used various Russian models, especially the T-26 with its 45 mm (1.77 in) gun. This was a much superior armament to the Panzer Is and IIs and the T-26 also enjoyed superior armor and durability. The Republican side got 281 or 297 of these models (sources vary) from the Soviet Union.

A T-26

The earliest versions of the T-26 had two turrets side by side, an odd feature found in several Interwar tanks that was soon discarded once the real fighting started. The classic single-turreted T-26 measured 4.55 m x 2.31 m x 2.30 m (14.93 x 7.58 x 7.55 ft), weighed 9.6 tons, had a maximum speed of 31 km/h (19 mph), a range of 240 km (150 mi) and 6 to 15 mm (0.24-0.59 in) thick armor. Its crew of three manned an effective 45 mm (1.77 in) gun and a single top-mounted 7.62 mm (.3 in) machine gun. This gun proved effective against armor, especially when firing a special armor-piercing round rather than the usual high explosive. One disadvantage was that only commander tanks had radios.

One of the great advantages of the T-26 was its simplicity of design and its relatively inexpensive price tag, so Soviet tank manufacturers were able to field about 10,000 of them by September 1939. The T-26 was the main Soviet tank of the 1930s and was used in the early years of World War II although by then it was gradually being replaced by more up-to-date models. Its thin armor and high profile made it vulnerable to tanks such as the Panzer III and IV, and any anti-gun bigger than the German PaK 36.

Early proof of the superiority of the Russian tanks in the Spanish Civil War was demonstrated at the Battle of Guadalajara in March 1937. The Nationalists, including a large number of Italian volunteers with L3/35 tankettes, made a thrust on Madrid, hoping to take the capital and bring a quick end to the war. They were stopped by the determined Republican resistance, aided by a number of T-26s that far outperformed the Italian tankettes armed only with their twin, hull-mounted machine guns. Many tankettes were destroyed and the attack on Madrid stalled.

The Spanish Civil War proved just how vulnerable tanks could be in the face of a determined defense. Both sides had anti-tank guns, the German 22 mm (8.66 in), 37 mm (1.46 in), and 47 mm (1.85 in) guns being reported as the most efficient. Even concentrated machine gun fire could knock out some of the more lightly armored models. Both sides became adept in digging tank traps, wide ditches that could not be crossed by even the largest tank and cut with steep sides to trap any tank unwary enough to fall in. Infantry also drenched tanks in gasoline and lit them on fire.

The most stunning act of anti-tank warfare was performed by the Republican Corporal Celestino Garcia Moreno, who came across a company of L3/35 tankettes packed in a city street. Armed with only several grenades and a pickaxe, the corporal managed to disable four tankettes, capture 10 men, and send the rest of the company into headlong retreat. If Señor Moreno had a few Ethiopian swordsmen along, he might have taken the entire company.

Heinz Guderian and the Development of Tank Doctrine

"The moral and intellectual condition of a nation may certainly prove of decisive importance on its own account, but all due attention must also be paid to material considerations. When a nation has to reckon with a struggle against superior forces on several fronts, it must neglect nothing that may conduce to the betterment of its situation." – Heinz Guderian

At the end of World War I, Germany was left crippled military, not only due to losses the nation had suffered while fighting but due to the terms of the Treaty of Versailles, responsible for ending the conflict. The treaty set strict rules in place, preventing Germany from employing certain tools of warfare, expanding its army beyond a specified size, or allowing for a general staffing group. Called the Reichswehr, the reduced army officially continued until 1935.

At the same time its army was being curtailed, the country was tearing itself apart where politics were concerned. The shock of defeat had unleashed extreme forces on both the right and left, and they all sought to take control of a bruised and battered Germany.

One obvious response to the Versailles limitations was to work on rearmament in secret. A general staff soon existed again in everything but name; using the innocuous title of the Truppenampt ("Troop Office"), it became a powerful faction within the military work on rearmament within the limits imposed by the Allies. The group, however, did not pursue a wider political agenda within Germany, as the Nazis would when they called for rearmament. Rather, these professional soldiers were concerned solely with military might. One of the leaders of this group was General Hans von Seekt, and a young officer named Heinz Guderian became one of von Seekt's loyal supporters and part of the effort to rebuild. Highly respected for his drive and intelligence, Guderian was found himself on the inside of the movement that would shape the German military until the 1930s.

General von Seekt

Guderian

Guderian's principle interest was in tanks. Having seen what this new technology could do, he wanted to make sure Germany had access to it, and he wanted his nation to be on the cutting edge of mechanized warfare.

As he shifted around Germany in various posts, Guderian kept reading extensively on the theory of tank warfare, especially the work coming out of Britain, the original home of the armored tank. His tank tactics were, at first, based on the ideas of British thinkers J.F.C. Fuller and Basil Liddell Hart, two men who had taken the lead developing the theory of tank warfare and keeping the British ahead of their competitors for years. Guderian read their works and the official British tank training manual, building upon them to create a German approach. He also kept track of the latest developments in Britain, where General Percy Hobart was experimenting with tank tactics, free from the same restrictions as Guderian. Guderian arranged for translations of Hobart's writings at his own expense.

Hobart

While the theoretical foundations of Guderian's tank tactics came from the West, the practical experience allowing him to develop the tactics came from the East. In 1922, Germany and Russia signed the Treaty of Rapallo. In public, the two nations were simply normalizing relations and giving up claims on each others' territories, but in secret, they began cooperating on developing their militaries, which created a golden opportunity for Guderian. The Germans had been banned from having an air force or tank formations, but in secret man oeuvres in Russia, they began to develop the exact same technologies and training the men to use them. Guderian was part of this work, taking part in exercises in Russia to develop tank tactics. In cooperation with German and Swedish manufacturers and the Russian military, he arranged for the production of prototypes for a range of different tanks.

One of Guderian's biggest interests was in ensuring communications between tanks. Having experience working with signals, he had seen how important good communication was in war and applied this experience, helping to develop secure radio communications between tanks that would allow them to coordinate their actions in battle. Communication with individual tanks was vital to the strategy he developed; for mechanized formations to strike deep into enemy territory, they had to be able to stay in contact securely at a distance. It took some time, but 1933 would see his ideas become a reality, as all German tanks began to be equipped with radios and a dedicated radio operator.

Guderian's lectures on mechanized warfare brought him publicity and support for his schemes, and his reforms and innovations impressed some of the military hierarchy. However, there was also a backlash. At times, Guderian struggled as much with the attitudes of the men around him as he did with the limitations imposed upon him by the peace treaty. He was convinced tanks were war-winning weapons of the future, but everyone did not share his views, and perhaps not surprisingly, old fashioned cavalry commanders were particularly resistant to the rise of the mechanized warfare threatening to make them obsolete. Guderian's blunt and argumentative approach, combined with his unusual ideas, singled him out as a maverick in the eyes of many generals.

In 1930, Guderian was transferred to take charge of a Motor Transport Battalion. He put together dummy versions of armored cars and tanks, vehicles the German army still couldn't technically possess, and put his battalion through all the maneuvers needed to fulfill his vision of fast-moving, armored warfare. It was a chance to refine his thinking and to prove that it could work. Slowly but surely, more and more German commanders came around to Guderian's point of view.

Meanwhile, rearmament was central to Hitler's political agenda once the Nazis took power. The restricted Reichswehr was renamed as the Wehrmacht, a larger, prouder, unrestrained collection of armed forces. As a part of this move, Hitler introduced conscription and announced the existence of an air force, two moves which broke the Treaty of Versailles and ended the illusion that Germany was still adhering to the treaty's terms. It was a provocative move, but one that was begrudgingly accepted by the international community. World War I was far behind them, the fear of German aggression fading into the past, but it would not take long for the irony of this attitude to be revealed.

As time went by, Guderian worked more and more closely with Hitler, and his first real chance to impress the new leader came in 1934, when Guderian, still only a colonel, was allowed to demonstrate his concept of the armored division in action. This involved coordinated activity across a wide range of troop types-reconnaissance cars, motorbikes, light tanks, artillery, and aircraft. Hitler was impressed, but he was already pouring most of his free resources into building the Luftwaffe. Progress with tanks remained slow and continued to frustrate Guderian, who had a particular vision for how Germany should fight, believing that tanks should be the principal weapons of war. Accompanied by motorized support troops on permanent attachment to tank formations, they would strike hard and fast against Germany's enemies. This was the vision he sold to Hitler, a vision which suited Hitler's desire for a dynamic, aggressive approach to both politics and war.

There were, however, problems. Failed experiments with tanks in Ethiopia and Spain made people wary of relying upon them, and despite the close connection he'd forged with the regime, Guderian struggled to gain support for his tank agenda.

Hitler marched German troops into the Rhineland in March of 1936, the first in a series of expansionist moves that would nudge Europe gradually toward war, and the Führer prepared his country for the coming conflict. He encouraged the military to develop a new approach to fighting, and Blitzkrieg was born. In August 1936, Guderian was made a major general. Given his rising career and Germany's military culture, it was the perfect environment for his ideas to take root.

Throughout his work, Guderian showed an aptitude for military theory, and in 1937, he put some of it into print in a book named *Achtung! Panzer!* In *Achtung! Panzer!*, Guderian assessed the state of armored warfare among the nations of Europe and the Soviet Union, based on his extensive studies. He argued that the era of cavalry was over due to the impact of machine-guns, and that mechanized infantry could be used to fill their role. He also set out his views with respect to the best way to conduct combined armored and armed warfare.

Guderian's approach as set out in *Achtung! Panzer!* was one of warfare by maneuver, in which speed and surprise were essential to victory. He couched his ideas in terms he knew would appeal to Hitler. Instead of committing them to protracted battles, he suggested commanders use panzer divisions in short, sharp operations in which timing was everything, orders were brief and to the point, and the attack came come swiftly, surprising the enemy before they had time to prepare a defense. Air support was to help tanks achieve the breakthroughs they needed. It was a tactic that would make tanks the heroes of the battlefield, rather than relegating them to the supporting role advocated by others. Central to this was the concentration of tanks in large masses, rather than spreading them out to support infantry units.

These ideas carried within them a reaction against World War I. After all, they aimed to avoid protracted and costly battles by preventing the preparation of defenses, rather than throwing men and resources to use against them. The idea of concentrating hard-hitting troops to achieve breakthroughs also built upon German tactics from late in World War I, when well-equipped stormtroopers had punched holes in the Allied lines and created a war of movement that briefly held out the promise of a German victory. The thinking wasn't entirely original, either in this or in Guderian's more specific approach to tanks, but it was still an important book by a leading thinker in his field. The continuity with Germany's past successes and the support of the Nazi machine only served to add to its appeal for many German officers.

Achtung! Panzer! wasn't a part of the official Nazi military doctrine, but it was published with official backing, and it fit well with the Nazi approach by focusing on strength, aggression, and radical approaches to problems. It showed a line of thinking in line with Hitler and the men who surrounded him. Hitler filled the Wehrmacht with officers sharing his ideas and with those who were eager to obey, in an effort to reduce the influence of the old guard.

Guderian was put in charge of XIX Corps in August 1939, which consisted of a panzer division and two divisions of motorized infantry. This assignment was perfect for carrying out the tactics he had been developing. As troops hurriedly maneuvered around Eastern Germany, the next target became clear.

They were about to invade Poland.

Blitzkrieg in Poland

Much has been said about Blitzkrieg tactics, but it must be remembered that the German army wasn't nearly as mechanized as films and some popular level books would have people believe. Many guns and supply wagons were still drawn by horses, and in numerous encounters the Germans found themselves short of armor. Nevertheless, the German integration of air, infantry, and armor was far superior to that of its early foes, and their armies moved much more quickly.

The idea of Blitzkrieg was to have a coordinated effort between tanks, other armored vehicles, motorized infantry, artillery, and aircraft to quickly establish an overwhelming local superiority to break through enemy lines. From there the vanguard pushed on rapidly to take major objectives while the slower, less mechanized forces to the rear performed mopping up operations. Local commanders were allowed a great deal of freedom to make on-the-spot decisions on how to complete their missions. In addition, every tank was equipped with a radio, something no other country had done. In other armies, tanks had to signal to each other with flags. Having a radio in every unit allowed German commanders to shift tactics at a moment's notice and also call in air strikes.

The Germans wouldn't bring this military doctrine into full effect until the invasion of France, but the invasion of Poland, while being a more traditional envelopment, would see the Nazis incorporate some aspects of Blitzkrieg.

Hitler had already annexed the Sudetenland in October 1938 and moved into the rest of Czechoslovakia on March 15, 1939. He had two main reasons for taking the country, one propagandistic and the other practical. First, he wanted to "liberate" the German-speaking minority in the country, and secondly he wanted the nation's heavy industry, most importantly its tank factories. Czechoslovakia had nearly 1,000 armored vehicles by the start of the war, many of them of better quality than the Panzer II and even the Panzer III. Besides various models of tankettes, already obsolete by the opening of hostilities, the main Czechoslovak models were the Škoda CKD LT vz. 35 and CKD vz. 38.

An LT-35

The Škoda CKD LT vz. 35 (Lehký tank vzor or "Light Tank Model"), designed in 1935, it measured 4.90 m × 2.06 m × 2.37 m (16.1 × 6.8 x 7.84 ft), weighed 10.5 tons, had 8 to 35 mm (0.3-1.4 in) armor depending on the surface, and a maximum speed of 34 km/h (21 mph). It had a crew of three (commander, driver, gunner) who manned a 37 mm (1.46 in) gun on the turret and two 7.92 mm (0.3 in) machine guns. The Škoda CKD LT vz. 35 was unusual among Interwar tanks outside of Germany in that each tank was provided with a radio, and more than 200 had been produced by the time of the Nazi invasion. The Germans were so impressed by the vehicle that they continued production of some 200 more under the name Panzerkampfwagen 35(t), the "t" standing for "Tschechich" (Czech). They served well in the Polish and French campaigns.

The Škoda LT vz.38 was designed to be a replacement to the Škoda CKD LT vz. 35, and it included a number of improvements, most notably a superior suspension system. It measured 4.60 m x 2.37 m x 2.25 m (15.09 x 7.78 x 7.38 ft), weighed 9.4 tons, a top speed of 42/15 km/h (26/9 mph), and 8 to 30 mm (0.31-1.18 in) armor. The crew of three (commander/gunner, driver, loader/radio operator) had the same armament as the previous model.

The first units were delivered on the eve of the German invasion and none were ready for service. The Germans tested and approved the design and dubbed them the Panzerkampfwagen 38(t). The turret was modified to make it roomier and allow for a fourth crewman. A total of 1,414 were produced. They constituted an important portion of the tanks during the invasions of Poland, Norway, and France, where their anti-tank capabilities were appreciated, and they also served in Operation Barbarossa, the invasion of the Soviet Union. By then, however, they were outmoded and suffered badly against Russian armor. The chassis became a popular platform for many variant tanks such as flamethrower tanks, flak guns, and self-propelled guns. This was a common German practice when tanks became outmoded, and the chasses of the Panzer I, II, and III all were refitted for various uses.

For the invasion of Poland, the Wehrmacht adopted a very bold, large-scale strategy, using two huge encircling movements to chop Polish territory into thirds. Army Group North, starting from East Prussia and northern Germany, launched two main thrusts southeast, while Army Group South, based in Germany and Czechoslovakia, launched two thrusts northwest. The Germans intended these pincer movements to converge at Warsaw and Brest-Litovsk, thereby cutting off and encircling vast numbers of Polish soldiers, who would be compelled to surrender or be annihilated.

For their part, the Poles predicated their strategy on fighting a delaying action in the west, accompanied by a slow withdrawal eastward. The Poles still believed the Soviets would not attack them; in fact, a few Polish leaders, more sanguine than the rest, thought the Russians might send aid to them to help expel the Germans. They also trusted their new alliance with the British and French to provide speedy relief. Both of these Polish hopes proved hollow.

Germany enjoyed a significant edge in tanks at 2,750, while the Poles could muster only 880. While many of the tanks were light Panzer Is and Czech 38(t) models, there were also many upgunned Panzer II tanks, plus tough, hard-hitting, medium-weight Panzer III models and even a handful of Panzer IVs. In contrast, 575 of Poland's tanks were actually 2.6 ton TKS and TK-3 tankettes, of which 551 carried no weaponry heavier than a machine-gun. The 24 tankettes built with 20mm cannons proved quite dangerous to German light (and sometimes medium) tanks, but these and the 305 battle tanks (light, poorly armed, feebly armored) the Poles fielded ultimately had no chance against Nazi armor.

At the start of the war, the Luftwaffe possessed 2,315 aircraft ready to deploy and slightly more than 4,000 in total. The Polish Air Force mustered just 400 obsolete fighters and no dive-bombers whatsoever. 9,000 advanced German artillery pieces, many towed by mechanical prime movers such as halftracks, matched up against 4,300 mostly horse-drawn field artillery and anti-tank artillery pieces, which were little more than World War I surplus. These guns proved sufficient to defeat the armor of Panzer I tanks, but they had more difficulty against thicker-armored later tank models such as Panzer II, Panzer III, and Panzer IV.

Technology and military doctrine both favored the Germans in the context of the era as well. The Germans considered communication key to good battlefield coordination and control, so radios were very commonplace. The Third Reich built large numbers of its tanks with individual radios, in contrast to the radio-free tanks of Poland. The Wehrmacht also made extensive use of radios in infantry units, and commanders, artillerymen, and spotters used radio communications to launch precise, timely fire missions to soften the way for their own attacks or halt those of the enemy.

Germany's army was far more mechanized than Poland's. Besides tanks and armored cars, a fleet of heavy trucks offered rapid transport of men and material. Halftracks moved artillery and ammunition to places where they were needed, and thousands of motorcycles with sidecars provided messenger service, scouting, and rapid deployment of machine gun teams. Statistics demonstrated the stark difference in mechanization between the opponents; 10% of the Polish army consisted of cavalry, while only 2% of the Wehrmacht was cavalry in 1939, a figure that was steadily shrinking too. Though a lack of fuel eventually proved the Achilles heel for German armies later in the war, this was not an issue during the Polish campaign of 1939.

In terms of doctrine, the Germans were years in advance of the Poles. Polish tanks were spread thin, assigned to supporting infantry units. The Germans clustered their armor assets into Panzer divisions which operated independently, striking rapidly and deeply into enemy territory and applying a concentration of force and firepower the Poles simply could not emulate with their diffuse armor deployments.

The Germans also utilized dive-bombers in the form of the famous Stuka. This aircraft made nearly vertical dives to deliver bombs precisely on target, enabling the rapid destruction of individual armored vehicles, squads or platoons of infantry, particular buildings (such as one housing an enemy command post or machine gun position), and so on. The Poles had no dive-bombers because they, like the other Allies, believed that the design was actually impossible, and that "anti-aircraft fire had reached such perfection that to dive below a certain level was tantamount to suicide and could not be contemplated. Again, the theory was sound, but in practice it required very steady nerves to stand at a gun while a line of dive-bombers was descending […] In practice, losses were few and the hits achieved by the dive-bomber were many." (Smith, 1998, 7).

German dive-bombers during the war

During the first week, the combat and deeply penetrating pincer movements rapidly degraded the ability of the Poles to keep resisting. The Polish air force, though gallant, died in flames where they crashed in the Polish countryside after being shot down by their German counterparts. Indeed, the Luftwaffe was the most elite arm of the Germany military at the start of the war, due in large part to the fact "they had the benefit of modern combat experience fed back from their *Legion Condor* contributions to the victory of General Franco's forces in Spain. In particular, many of the theories of army cooperation and close air support were put to the practical test and invaluable lessons absorbed." (Smith, 1998, 5). The Polish soldiers soon learned that venturing out onto roads in daylight was certain death, as any column of Polish infantry, cavalry, or vehicles was soon spotted by the Germans. Using their radios, the Wehrmacht called in the location to the Luftwaffe, whose terrible dive-bombers soon appeared to spread slaughter among the men trapped in the flat, open Polish countryside under the light of day.

With so many disadvantages weighing against them, the Poles could not maintain their defense for more than a few days, regardless of their courage and occasional local successes. Within four to five days, Polish command at all levels lost communications contact with both headquarters and with other Polish formations elsewhere in the country. Given this lack of strategic coordination, the Poles found themselves fighting blind against a highly coordinated foe whose command of the skies gave them almost total information regarding troop movements and strategic developments. "The dam burst: German mechanised columns plunged deep into Polish lines, and on 7 September the tanks of the 4th Panzer Division began appearing outside the suburbs of Warsaw. They began immediately to make attempts to break into the city itself, but showed little judgement, and on 9 September alone the Poles claimed 57 tanks from the 4th Panzer Division in intense street fighting. The second week of the war went just as badly." (Zaloga, 1982, 10).

By September 20, Poland's armies were effectively defeated in both the west and the east. Warsaw held out heroically for some time, but by October 6, the nation of Poland had all but ceased to exist. It now only remained for the victorious Nazis and Soviets to divide up the spoils and decide what was to be done with the unfortunate population. Poland, which had emerged from centuries of servitude in the wake of World War I, had found itself subjected to foreign conquerors again in 1939. Indeed, the men who now ruled its fate were far crueler than any who had come over its borders since the days of the Mongol hordes.

A picture of German and Soviet soldiers shaking hands in Poland

In the west, Britain and France had declared war on Germany, but they ultimately did nothing to aid their Polish allies. Their promises to hasten to the Poles' assistance in the event of foreign attack proved to be worth no more than the breath expended speaking them and the paper they were written on. The French advanced a few miles into Germany, seizing some unoccupied forest, but French soldiers refused to move outside the range of the artillery mounted in the Maginot Line, even though nearly every German soldier was redeployed hundreds of miles to the east.

The French command noted that Hitler's new method of warfare was nearly "Napoleonic" in its nature and further added, "The frontline does not exist any more and is replaced by a three-dimensional space extending on all the territory occupied by the fighting armies. Consequently the linear disposition of the troops along the frontier seems to appear totally wrong [. . .] The vital forces of the enemy have to be gradually destroyed. Their blows have to be answered by blows [. . .] The fight should be carried by independent groups of great units." (Williamson, 2009, 195).

However, despite clearly realizing (and even enunciating) this, the French acted in precisely the opposite manner by putting their full faith in a linear disposition of troops along the frontier and in fixed fortifications. A few days after venturing unwillingly over the border into Germany, the "Gallic cockerel" scuttled back ignominiously to the relative safety of the French border defenses, where the French would await their own turn on the chopping block of Hitler's insatiable aggression. With that feeble gesture, the attempts of the British and French to come to the aid of Poles abruptly ended.

Despite the stunning victory against the Poles, the Germans suffered some serious casualties against a much weaker nation that was simultaneously fighting a war with the Soviet Union. German casualties are a matter of dispute, but most historians believe that they lost about 40,000 killed and wounded plus some 800 tanks. Considering the entire invading force had only 2,750 tanks, this was an unacceptably high figure. Granted, this figure includes breakdowns, but weak armor was the most to blame, as well as the bravery of the Polish gun and tank crews. Fortunately for the German war effort, the majority of these tanks could be repaired and brought back into service.

French Tanks

The Germans would obviously face a stronger foe in France in 1940. The French had a total of 6,126 tanks. About a quarter of them were outmoded FT-17s from the early Interwar period, and its outmoded update, the FT-31. The French also had four powerful tank models that proved more than a match against all but the Panzer IV, and they occasionally proved equal to even that powerful tank. The French had been constantly testing tanks during the Interwar period, and this had led to the introduction of a new series of heavier tanks that were some of the best to be fielded at the beginning of the war. There were also several models that saw limited production that are beyond the scope of this work.

The Hotchkiss corporation produced the H35, meant as a light tank that could be easily mass produced and act as infantry support. The Hotchkiss H35 was a true innovation, being the first tank to have its armor sections entirely cast rather than being plates riveted together. This gave added strength because there were fewer seams. The hull was made up of only three cast sections welded together and the turret was a single piece. This technique reduced the chance for spalling—bits of metal on the interior shearing off from impact on the exterior and ripping through the compartment. Later in the war, casting became standard for many tanks.

An abandoned Hotchkiss H35

The H35 measured 4.22 m x 1.95 m x 2.15 m (13.1 x 10.6 x 5.7 ft) with 25-40 mm (0.98-1.57 in) armor. It had a maximum speed of 28 km/h (17 mph) and a range of only 130 km (80 mi). It weighed a fairly light 9.6 tons. Its two-man crew (driver, commander/gunner) used a 37 mm (1.46 in) short-barrel gun and a coaxial 7.5 mm (0.295 in) machine gun.

The H39 update incorporated a more powerful engine that brought the top speed to 36.5 km/h (22.6 mph) and a larger gas tank that upped the range to 150 km (93 mi). A few were fitted with a more powerful, longer-barreled 37 mm (1.46 in) gun with better penetration power, but these were in short supply.

A total of 1,200 H35/39s were produced, most of which were available to the French during the invasion. Slow and undergunned, they did not do well during the invasion despite the fact their thick armor easily deflected the PaK 36 37 mm (1.46 in) German infantry gun, the main infantry anti-tank gun the Germans had.

The SOMUA S35 was also entirely cast. It differed from the H35 in that it was a "cavalry" tank, meant to perform the traditional duties of the cavalry by pushing through gaps in the enemy line to hit rear areas. Thus it needed a better range and speed, as well as thicker armor in order to deal with anti-tank fire. It measured 5.38 m x 2.12 m x 2.62 m (17.65 x 6.96 x 8.96 ft), weighed 19.5 tons, a maximum speed of 40 km/h (25 mph), a range of 230 km (142 mi), and armor ranging from 20 to 48 mm (0.7-1.8 in). Its three-man crew (driver, commander, gunner) served a 47 mm (1.85 in) gun and two 7.5 mm (0.295 in) machine guns. One machine gun was coaxial with the main gun. They were all supposed to be supplied with radios but production delays meant that only one in five ever carried one. Only 430 units were completed by June 1940. The SOMUA S35 performed well in one-on-one engagements against the Panzers, with its gun proving deadly, but like all other tanks, it would fall victim to poor French tactics and command structure.

A picture of SOMUA S35s captured by the Germans

The Renault R35/40 was the Renault company's answer to the Hotchkiss H35 and quite similar in many details. It was, like the Hotchkiss model, an "infantry" tank and its armor was cast instead of rivetted. The tank measured 4.02 m x 1.87 m x 2.13 m (13.2 x 6.2 x 7 ft) and measured 10.6 metric tons. The crew of two (driver and commander/gunner) served a 37 mm (1.46 in) short-barreled gun and a coaxial 7.5 mm (0.29 in) machine gun. This underpowered main gun could penetrate a maximum of only 12 mm (0.47 in) of armor, and to do that had to be closer than 500 m (1640 ft). Thus it could only take out the frontal armor of the Panzer I, and that assuming that the Panzers let it get close enough to try. Its own armor had a maximum thickness of 43 mm (1.69 in), making it impervious to most German guns. The R35 had a top speed of 20 km/h (12.4 mph), and considerably slower on difficult terrain, and a range of only 130 km (80 mi). This made it far inferior to the Panzers. It also suffered from a poorly designed suspension that often broke down.

A Renault R35

Considering all these failings, a new model was soon ordered. The R40 had an improved suspension, and carried a long-barreled SA38 37 mm (1.46 in) gun better suited to take out tanks. The shell could penetrate up to 40 mm (1.57 in) of armor at 500 m (1640 ft), thus being able to take out the front armor of the early model Panzer III. The tank was better protected than most of its opponents with up to 60 mm (2.36 in) of armor. All units included a radio.

A total of 900 of the R35s were available at the outbreak of the war, and a few of the later R40 models made it into service in time to face the Panzers. A large number of R35s were captured in the German invasion. Some were used as-is, while others were modified as tank hunters by fitting them with larger guns, and some were given to Italy.

The Char B1 bis was France's heaviest tank, designed to take out fortifications and enemy tanks. It measured 6.37 m x 2.46 m x 2.79 m (20.8 x 8.07 x 9.15 ft). It had a crew of four: commander, driver, main and secondary gunner. Its 47 mm (1.85 in) gun was an effective tank killer. It also had a 7.5 mm (0.295 in) machine gun. It had a maximum armor of 60 mm (2.36 in) and weighed a hefty 28 tons. It had a maximum speed of 28 km/h (17 mph) and a range of 200 km (120 mi). Each unit was fitted with a radio.

The Char B1 bis

The B1 bis proved highly effective against German armor. During the Stonne counteroffensive, a single B1 bis, the *Eure*, commanded by Captain Pierre Billotte, took out 13 Panzer IIIs and IVs while taking no fewer than 140 hits that merely bounced off its armor. The *Eure* was able to withdraw at the end of the fight. Only the Panzer IV had a gun strong enough to pierce the B1 bis's armor, and only at near point-blank range. Standard German anti-tank guns such as the PaK 37 and PaK 40 were similarly ineffective. Unfortunately for the French, only about 340 of this model were available at the time of the invasion, and captured B1 bis tanks would subsequently be used by the Germans to great effect in the Balkans and on the Eastern Front.

All French tanks suffered from the disadvantage that the commander was also given the task of manning the gun, and often had to load the gun and man the machine gun as well. This made him overworked and incapable of keeping a sharp eye on his surroundings. Time and again, Panzers would surprise French tanks, and this problem could not be solved by putting a second man in the turret because the casting techniques of the day limited the turret's size.

In the end, the main German advantages would lie not in any technological advance but in superior speed, tactics, and command and control. French tanks were spread out among infantry units as support and lacked radios, and orders came from the top with subordinates having little freedom of discretion. The slow speed of most French tanks was not seen as a problem since they moved with the infantry, and this also allowed for thicker armor. The low-velocity guns were meant more to take out pillboxes and other fortifications than opposing tanks. German forces moved quickly enough that they often took the French off-guard. While the smaller Panzers couldn't face off against the French main tanks, they proved adept at luring them into range of German anti-tank units. The slow speed and narrow range of many French models meant they got encircled or ran out of gas. Advancing German columns often found entire tank units abandoned by the side of the road, in perfect condition except for their empty gas tanks.

The Panzers had the added advantage of being able to radio in to the Luftwaffe to request airstrikes. When Guderian was rushing towards the English Channel to cut off the British Expeditionary Force, his advance units never had to wait more than 20 minutes between calling for an airstrike and seeing the dive bombers overhead.

The Conquest of Belgium and France

The first decisive encounters of the German invasion of France in 1940 occurred not on French but on Belgian soil. As the strategy behind the Maginot Line made clear, French planning and strategy not only anticipated this but encouraged it in an effort to keep the Third Reich's military forces off French soil. Much of France's key industrial might operated on the northern coastal plain, so retaining this manufacturing capacity gave the French a better chance to win the conflict, remaining able to replace equipment losses rapidly. Seizure of the area would constitute a major prize for the Germans. Of course, the Belgians were far less enthusiastic about the scheme, which transformed their small country into a battlefield on which two larger nations would unleash the full fury of modern bombing, strafing, and tank warfare.

As France hoped, the Maginot Line channeled the Germans much as intended until later breakthroughs made it moot, and it actually succeeded in halting Italian dictator Benito Mussolini's massive invasion force in its tracks in southeast France. However, by that point, the French strategy suffered a crippling blow as a result of Belgian neutrality.

The German plan, *"Fall Gelb,"* involved sending 28 divisions under General Fedor von Bock, grouped into "Army Group B," into Belgium, but this group could not penetrate into the Belgian interior unless several strategic bridges over the Meuse River and the Albert Canal fell rapidly into German hands. Fort Eben-Emael commanded the approach to these bridges, so the German OKW (high command) made its immediate capture the vital first objective of the entire campaign.

Von Bock

Under the German plan, Eben-Emael's capture would open the door to Army Group B's swift advance into Belgium proper. The OKW expected French and British forces to pour into Belgium from the west to counterattack Army Group B, so when this occurred, Army Group A – consisting of 7 panzer divisions and 37 other divisions – would attack through the weakly defended Ardennes Forest, break through near Sedan, and circle up towards the coast, thereby trapping the majority of the French and British armies in Belgium and cutting them off from supplies. At that point, the Germans figured their surrender would follow swiftly.

Hitler, in one of his rare moments of tactical lucidity, decided to use a revolutionary method to seize Eben-Emael quickly. A force of paratroopers and combat engineers would land on the fortress using gliders and blow its formidable defenses to pieces with the German Army's new secret siege weapon: the hollow-charge explosive. A force of hand-picked men received intensive, secretive training in this assault from late 1939 through March 1940. Dubbed "Sturmabteilung Koch" after their commander, Hauptmann Walter Koch, these men trained intensively in utter secrecy, to the extent that the Wehrmacht executed two of them by firing squad merely for revealing their presence at a nearby base to some local young women. The Sturmabteilung consisted of four Sturmgruppe; the OKW assigned one, "Sturmgruppe Granit" ("Granite"), to take Eben-Emael, while Sturmgruppe Beton, Stahl, and Eisen (Concrete, Steel, and Iron) would simultaneously seize three key bridges.

Koch

The Germans tested and refined every detail of their brand new tactical system, until the men could land within 60 feet of a designated aiming point every time: "[T]rials of glider landings on a simulated area of Fort Eben Emael revealed that the DFS 230 required a longer stopping distance than was available, especially when landing on wet grass that was only to be expected with the dawn dew. Modifications were made by incorporating a wooden drag brake beneath the glider that dug into the ground on landing." (Dunstan, 2005, 38).

The Allies ignored several indications of a coming attack, including a French pilot reporting seeing a column of armored vehicles tens of miles long snaking ominously through the countryside towards the Ardennes Forest like a steel dragon on May 7, 1940. Warnings of an impending German attack also circulated on May 9, including a message from Pope Pius XII himself, but the alert failed to reach Eben-Emael until early on May 10, a few short hours before the attack.

Luftwaffe air support formed a key part of the *Fall Gelb* plan in all of its particulars. A fighter "umbrella" guarded the huge Panzer army moving towards the Ardennes forest and the weak point at Sedan, and air power supported the push into Belgium and broke up Belgian counterattacks against the bridgeheads across various rivers.

The German feint by Army Group B, the so-called "Matador's Cloak," proved to be a smashing success. In response, the whole British Expeditionary Force (BEF), plus two French armies – the 1ere and 7ere – shifted into Belgium, putting them in a perfect position to be cut off by Army Group A's *Schwerpunkt* (main assault) through the Ardennes and the weakly held lines near Sedan.

World War II's first major tank battle developed at Hannut as the Germans and French maneuvered for tactical supremacy in the Belgian countryside. Given how the rest of the campaign turned out, it's little surprise the Battle of Hannut is largely forgotten today, but it stood out at the time as a notable French success as their tanks severely bloodied the nose of the advancing Germans and destroyed a number of Wehrmacht armored vehicles during a struggle lasting several days and involving hundreds of tanks on each side.

A picture of German soldiers inspecting disabled tanks at Hannut

As May 12 dawned, the Belgian I, II, III, and Cavalry Corps held the northern 30 miles of the line, while the BEF occupied the center and the French 1ere Army held the south between Warve and the Meuse River valley. It was here that General Rene Prioux's two armored divisions found themselves confronted by German panzers under the warm spring sunlight of a late Belgian morning. Lt. Robert Le Bel described it as "an extraordinary show which was played out about three kilometres [2 miles] away: a panzer division shaping itself for battle. The massive gathering of this armoured armada was an unforgettable sight, the more so that it appeared even more terrifying through the glasses..Some men, probably officers, walked to and fro gesticulating in front of the tanks. They were probably giving last-minute orders." (Evans, 2000, 46).

The French deployed SOMUA S-35 tanks with 47mm guns capable of piercing early-war German tank armor at most combat ranges and armor thick enough to provide cover against the main guns of 1940 variants of Panzer III and Panzer IV medium tanks. The weakness of the SOMUA lay in its one-man turret, which forced the commander to occupy multiple roles and thus reduced overall crew efficiency.

A SOMA S-35 captured by the Germans

A Panzer IV

Alongside these, the French used an equal number of Hotchkiss H-39 light tanks, armed with a 37mm gun capable of engaging German armored vehicles only at close ranges due to weak penetration against tank armor. Each division fielded 88 SOMUA S-35s and 87 Hotchkiss H-39s, the latter a stopgap due to insufficient supplies of SOMUAs.

For their part, the Germans deployed Panzer IIIs and Panzer IVs against the French, supported by the light Panzer I and Panzer II tanks with their flimsy armor and weak firepower. Supporting these, however, the Luftwaffe fielded the deadly Stuka dive-bombers, whose characteristic rising howl while diving, created by purpose-built sirens, often caused panic among those it targeted.

The Germans moved forward with four Panzer regiments deployed abreast, with 20 Panzer IIIs leading and 12 Panzer IVs backing them up while 48 Panzer Is and IIs guarded the flanks. The French near Hannut faced 80 Panzer IIIs, 48 Panzer IVs, and 192 lighter Panzers along a 22-mile front. Each side also deployed armored cars, which chiefly served a scouting role but also skirmished viciously with one another. The Germans also held motorized infantry in reserve.

Prioux chose his ground well – the Hannut area, 18 miles east of the Dyle Line, consists of "tank country," gently rolling hills with numerous scattered groves and small clumps of forest, and hamlets to provide cover. The centerpiece of his defense consisted of a long, low ridge providing good fields of fire. Lt. Robert Le Bel's tank, from which he saw the ominous sight of the German tanks deploying, occupied a position at the heart of the French defenses, around Hannut itself. Here, sheltered by walls, hedges, and clumps of trees, the SOMUAs and Hotchkiss tanks lurked, awaiting the onslaught.

At first, the French soldiers saw nothing but an undulating cloud of dust kicked up by the treads of hundreds of tank tracks, flowing across the landscape towards them. Then the boxy shapes of tanks loomed out of the beige haze, and the French opened fire. The French tanks inflicted high casualties against the Panzer I and II tanks. At one point, a German tank commander from one of the knocked out tanks ran forward in a frenzy of frustrated rage and clambered atop a Hotchkiss tank, swinging a hammer he perhaps meant to use on its periscope. However, he missed his footing and tumbled off, crushed to death a moment later under the tank's track.

The Germans launched a strong attack on the village of Crehen and took it, driving out the French tanks and infantry. They subsequently moved on to attack Thisnes shortly after noon, and the hard-hitting Panzer IIIs and Panzer IVs destroyed 13 of the lighter Hotchkiss tanks defending Thisnes, forcing the rest to pull back.

However, at 5:30 p.m., the deep, throbbing growl of tank engines announced the approach of a French counterattack. These armored vehicles, formidable SOMUA S-35s, rolled forward, sending rounds from their 47mm guns punching through armor plates and turning panzers into shattered hulks. The battle raged fiercely until 8:30 p.m., at which point the Germans withdrew from both Crehen and Thisnes, though they destroyed four SOMUA S-35s during the fighting. The day ended with the French holding their static defense line along the Hannut ridge.

On May 13, the German commander concentrated his panzers for two narrow-front attacks designed to penetrate the French line. In the north, Horst Stumpff's 3rd Panzer Division struck at Orp-le-Grand and Orp-le-Petit, but recoiled in the face savage French counterattacks, leaving the gently rolling farmland dotted with burning wrecks. After that, Stumpff sent in his supporting infantry, and a brutal gunbattle erupted between French and German foot soldiers, neither willing to give an inch of ground to the other.

At 3:20 p.m., the 5th and 6th panzer regiments attempted another penetration, but the French, responding with commendable aggression, struck at these panzer thrusts with tank attacks of their own. The Germans called the concentrated tank melee a "Hexenkessel," or "witches' cauldron."

To the south, Johann Stever led 250 panzers of the 4th Panzer Division against the village of Merdorp, but the Germans initially enjoyed no better success than Stumpff. French armor and artillery flung his attacking forces back with heavy losses. Eventually, however, Stever's persistent attacks cut down on the numbers of surviving French tanks, and at approximately 3:00 p.m., the last two Hotchkiss tanks and 10 SOMUAs broke out westward, leaving Merdorp in Stever's hands.

May 13 witnessed additional "Hexenkessel" battles at Jandrain and Jauche. The Germans deployed their heaviest tanks, Panzer IIIs and IVs, in large numbers at these points. At Jandrain, Eberbach's panzers finally managed to destroy 8 SOMUA S-35 tanks, while the crews abandoned five more, permitting their capture. At Jauche, five remaining French tanks retreated, proving impervious to German tank gun fire. The group included Lt. Robert Le Bel: "According to the panzers' war diary, 'Fire was opened on every one of these moving tanks by PzR 6 and the PaK Kompanie, so that every tank took a large number of hits, including 7.5cm high-explosive rounds. None of the French tanks was penetrated and put out of action.' After the battle, le Bel's Hotchkiss showed impact marks from being hit by 15 A/T rounds and 42 bullets." (Dildy (2), 2015, 89).

The French armor disengaged and fell back, largely under cover of night. Prioux still had fight left in him, however. He formed a new defensive line 5.5 miles west of the Hannut line, positioning his tanks in ambush at the edge of a forest overlooking the Belgian steel "tank fences." On May 14, the Germans penetrated the fence at Perwez and fell into the French ambush. Prioux's tanks continued to crush repeated panzer attacks from 10:30 a.m. until the afternoon, when the French again withdrew.

On the following day, the Germans found themselves halted by French tanks once again near Gembloux. May 15 saw the last large-scale armored action in Belgium, however. The French high command split up Prioux's remaining tanks among the infantry, rendering them effectively useless, but at a cost of 40 SOMUAs and 94 Hotchkiss tanks, the French knocked out 222 panzers, with 48 totally destroyed and 174 crippled, thus slowing the German advance to a crawl for a remarkable span of five days.

The Battle of Hannut proved to German tank commanders that while their tactics, organization, and combined use of all branches of service could lead to victory, most of their tanks were too weak. The SOMUA S35s could beat any German tank and were invulnerable to the Panzer Is and IIs. Even the Panzer III had to be at a dangerously close range to have any hope of knocking it out. At Hannut, the Germans enjoyed numerical superiority in men and artillery plus overwhelming air superiority but only managed to fight the French to a draw. It was essential that the Panzers be improved. The losses in the fight for France would spur on production of the Panzer IV and encourage development of even more robust models. They also learned not to send their tanks forward without infantry support. The Allies learned the bitter lesson that they needed to have better command and control—a more unified system of moving tanks and radios in every unit. The static fighting of World War I was a thing of the past. One French tank commander complained that during the battle he had to leap out of his tank, rush over to those of his fellow tankers, and pound on the hatches in order to give orders. Another French commander made the common complaint that being alone in the turret that he was overburdened with responsibilities, and that once he started firing his gun, he lost command over his platoon.

The Battle of Hannut provided a grimly spectacular introduction to the age of tank warfare and represented perhaps the finest success of the French military during the invasion, but while Army Group B drew the Allies into Belgium and suffered a notable check at the Battle of Hannut, Army Group A hastened forward to complete the doom of Western Europe. 41,000 vehicles of all kinds, including numerous panzers, plus SdKfz armored cars, trucks, motorcycles, self-propelled guns, and other machines, moved through Luxembourg and entered the Ardennes Forest to strike at the weak point in the French line near Sedan. Sedan lay between the Allied armies in the north and the start of the Maginot Line, held only by poor quality reserve units.

Remarkably, the overall French commander, Maurice Gamelin, knew of the German movement through the Ardennes from the beginning. His reconnaissance pilots did their work well, bringing him reports of large numbers of tanks snaking along the Ardennes' winding roads. However, Gamelin dismissed these as a "rather violent feint" and continued to operate on the stubborn belief that Belgium represented the main theater of war, largely based on assumed parallels to World War I.

Nevertheless, the 1,222 Panzers and supporting vehicles advanced at remarkable speed. To cut sleep to a minimum, Guderian issued pervitin amphetamines to his men, drugs given the nickname "panzer chocolate" by the men of the Heer. This early version of "crystal meth" allowed long periods of being awake and imparted a euphoric mood, but at the risk of heart attacks, suicide, psychotic violence, or a collapse into addiction.

The Wehrmacht's advance through the Ardennes only met opposition from scattered Allied forces. In the north, the Belgian Keyaerts Group, including the Chasseurs Ardennais, put up a "spirited resistance" before withdrawing to the north to rejoin the main Belgian forces on the Dyle Line, and in the south, the Germans encountered and quickly routed units of French horsed cavalry, using both armored attacks and Stuka dive-bomber strikes to disperse the lightly armed defenders. (Thomas, 2014, 31).

The Germans arrived at the Meuse on May 12 largely free from harassment by Franco-British aircraft and were confronted by relatively weak defenses. Standing on the bank of the Meuse, Fedor von Bock confided to his diary, "Concerning Army Group A, the 4th Army has succeeded in crossing the Meuse near Yvoir and Dinant and has established bridgeheads there. The French really do seem to have taken leave of their senses." (Healy, 2008, 45). On May 13, Guderian's panzers crossed the Meuse almost unopposed, and the Germans launched a colossal Stuka dive-bomber attack of 500 sorties against the 55e Reserve Regiment, a low-quality French unit guarding the river near Sedan. General Maurice Gamelin, proving himself once again completely unfit to hold command, responded to requests for anti-aircraft guns to be sent to aid the 55e Regiment with the airy response that their squad machine guns would suffice to drive the Stukas away. These weapons, of course, lacked the range, accuracy, or striking power to even inconvenience the swiftly-descending Luftwaffe dive-bombers.

The stunned French found themselves under fire from the east bank by the deadly 88mm flak cannon, a German anti-aircraft gun which proved equally lethal against bunkers, buildings, and practically every type of armored vehicle fielded by the Allies during World War II. Guderian himself used a rubber assault boat to cross the Meuse after troops and engineers established a foothold on the west bank, and his subordinate, Lieutenant Colonel Balck, met him with a bit of jubilant, good-natured cheekiness as his boat approached shore. "He greeted me cheerfully with the cry 'Joy-riding in canoes on the Meuse is forbidden!' I had in fact used those words myself in one of the exercises that we had in preparation for this operation, since the attitude of some of younger officers had struck me as rather too light-hearted. I now realized that they had judged the situation correctly." (Evans, 2000, 52). Guderian's engineers threw three pontoon bridges across the Meuse at Wadelincourt, Glaire, and Donchery, and by midnight on the 13th, panzers poured across these temporary but expertly constructed bridges and moved on into the French countryside.

Meanwhile, Rommel's men arrived at the Meuse near Houx, a village close to Dinant, after fighting through unexpectedly stiff resistance on the eastern bank. Scouting carefully, the Germans found a long-abandoned weir connecting the two banks by way of a forested island in midstream. Waiting for complete darkness, a unit of German motorcycle troops drove their vehicles slowly across the river on the weir, establishing a bridgehead on the west bank. Though the French counterattacked strongly the next day with machine guns and mortar fire, the motorcycle soldiers maintained their foothold. Rommel's engineers rigged a cable ferry using pontoon boats intended for building a bridge, which allowed more infantry and armored vehicles to cross the Meuse, leading to expansion of the German foothold on the west bank and the eventual construction of complete pontoon bridges.

The second and last major tank battle of Germany's 1940 French campaign developed at Stonne near the Sedan crossings. Here, the most deadly French tank of the time, the strangely constructed Char B1 Bis, formed the core of French resistance. Armed with a 47mm gun in its turret and a second 75mm gun bizarrely mounted in its hull, the Char B1 Bis featured 60mm armor on most surfaces, which provided protection against early German tank guns and most towed anti-tank guns also.

A disabled Char B1 Bis

One Char B1 bis, dubbed "Joan of Arc," demonstrated this near-invulnerability when it engaged a large number of German AT guns supported by light vehicles. The tank knocked out two armored cars, but eventually lost its guns to concentrated enemy fire. Nevertheless, it survived more than 90 direct hits, many at point-blank range, while actually running over and crushing approximately 25 Wehrmacht AT guns in succession. Only a lucky shot through the side radiator port finally put a stop to Joan of Arc's rampage. On another occasion, a Char B1 bis survived 160 direct hits.

Stonne stood on a plateau 9 miles south of Sedan, and both sides recognized it as a key point in the struggle for the Meuse bridgeheads. The French wanted to assemble a counterattack against the German crossing here, while the Wehrmacht was intent on seizing the town and plateau to forestall precisely this maneuver.

The tank expert Jean Flavigny led the French 21e Corps during the action, and the French were pitted against the 10th Panzer Division, supported by the Grossdeutschland Infantry Division. The French overall regional commander, Charles Huntziger, gave Flavigny two sets of orders, one offensive (retake Sedan) and the other defensive (hold Stonne). Flavigny had 53 Char 1B bis at his disposal, but their supporting motorized infantry remained absent, delayed on the traffic-clogged roads. Accordingly, Flavigny opted to stay on the defensive and let the panzers come to him.

At 5:00 a.m. on May 15, shortly after a brief German artillery barrage struck Stonne, a column of 11 German tanks moved upslope towards the town and around the hairpin bend at the top. Six Panzer IV tanks led, with five lighter Panzer II tanks backing them up. As the Germans rounded the corner with the houses and church of Stonne in sight ahead, a sharp report punctured the morning air, and the lead Panzer IV slowed to a stop. A 25mm French anti-tank gun, commanded by the grizzled veteran Sergeant Durand, coolly fired several more shots into the lead tank, ensuring its disablement. The second panzer suffered a similar fate, while the third perished in more spectacular fashion by exploding violently.

The remaining panzers pushed forward nevertheless, forcing the French to pull back and form a temporary defensive line just south of Stonne. This signaled the start of a prolonged, seesaw combat in which Stonne changed hands no less than 17 times over the course of May 15-16. During the fighting, the German tanks fired so many shots at the nearly impregnable Char B1 bis tanks that crews often abandoned their vehicles temporarily to scavenge unused shells from nearby knocked-out panzers. Feldwebel Karl Koch provided a vivid glimpse of this fighting: "After a while, a fourth tank appeared through the orchard. It was a real monster and we had no idea that France had tanks like that. We fired 20 shots at it without success. However, after a few more shots, we managed to knock off its track. [...] a fifth tank appears, another B1 firing all its weapons. [...] We fired, but could not knock it out until a ricochet hit the turret. The next shot hit it in the rear. Calm returned and we abandoned our tank again because we had exhausted the ammunition." (Zaloga, 2011, 67).

The battle turned into an infantry combat late on the 15th, but after massive French artillery strikes before dawn on May 16th, both sides committed their remaining tanks to a fresh armored encounter. Captain Pierre Billotte, France's premier Char B1 bis tank ace – destined to survive the war, found an important labor union, and die many years later at the start of the Internet era in 1992 – now entered the fray. After knocking out one tank leading the German armor thrust, Billotte described what happened next: "The panzers following it were spaced at regular intervals on a 200-metre climb, each of them being shielded by those in front. On the other hand, I was uphill and I could fire at them from above…In ten minutes, the panzers at the head of the column were all silenced, one after the other, and I could see the ones in the rear hastily withdrawing." (Evans, 2000, 64). Billotte knocked out at least 9 and perhaps as many as 13 panzers in his attack, all without losing his own tank, "Eure."

Another French tank commander, Lieutenant Doumercq, earned a different type of fame when he cornered a German infantry platoon and crushed a number of men to death under his Char B1 Bis' tracks. Horrified by this action, both the French and Germans took to calling Doumercq "the Butcher of Stonne."

At the end of the ferocious tank fighting on May 16th, both sides withdrew their armored forces from the area around Stonne. The infantry continued to maul each other until the 23rd in a miniature reprise of World War I trench warfare, at which point the French finally withdrew and left the powdered rubble of Stonne to the Wehrmacht.

After the Germans had forced the Meuse crossings OKW, the Wehrmacht high command, ordered Guderian to halt the Germans for 24 hours to give them time to rest, regroup, and refuel. However, Guderian decided to deliberately and thoroughly flout these orders; having gained a stunning advantage over the French, he declined to sacrifice it even to give his soldiers and himself much-needed rest. Guderian rightly figured that only by keeping up the pressure could the Panzer Divisions exploit the opportunities offered by running amok in the Allied rear.

Rommel found himself in the lead on May 15th, driving in his Kubelwagen staff car alongside much better protected panzers. The Germans pushed west and took a curving path northwest as they punched deep into French territory, aiming to reach the coast of the English Channel. In this way, the Wehrmacht would encircle the BEF and much of the French Army deployed in Belgium, putting them in an untenable position and hopefully forcing their surrender.

The Germans used forests – cleared of undergrowth for firewood like most European woodland at the time and therefore offering scant obstacle to tracked vehicles – to avoid air attacks, while bypassing towns where soldiers and anti-tank guns might delay their advance. Rommel pushed out far ahead of the main force but paused on a hill crest near sunset on May 15th to survey the landscape to his rear: "Looking back east from the summit of the hill, as night fell, endless pillars of dust could be seen rising as far as the eye could reach — comforting signs that the 7th Panzer Divisions move into the conquered territory had begun." (Evans, 2000, 70).

Rommel and Guderian continued their drive on the 16th, and the French forces showed strong signs of panic as the Germans pierced ever deeper into France. Many men encountered by the

Wehrmacht made no effort to attack them, instead streaming down side roads in an attempt to escape. The Germans brushed past these and moved on as the French Army assumed the role of a traffic hazard rather than an active enemy force.

At this point, the OKW nearly scuppered the successful blitzkrieg from within. Field Marshal Paul von Kleist – eventually killed by the Russians for the crime of "alienating, through friendship and generosity, the peoples of the Soviet Union" – ordered Guderian to halt, fearing the overextended German advance would suffer counterattack and annihilation. Guderian tendered his resignation, thinking this would overcome Kleist's objections, but to his astonishment, Kleist accepted it. Ultimately, Gerd von Rundstedt adroitly averted this potential crisis of command by intervening with a solution; Rundstedt's plan called for Guderian to halt but permitted him to make a "reconnaissance in force." Rundstedt left the size and nature of this "reconnaissance" totally undefined, effectively writing Guderian a blank check to do whatever he wished so long as he made the conciliatory gesture of establishing a fixed headquarters and remaining there for a while.

On May 16th, the French command sent Colonel Charles de Gaulle to make a flanking attack with a tank force on the rapidly growing German salient. This, however, was too little, too late. De Gaulle found himself commanding a pitifully small force of tanks, but he nevertheless made a brave attempt to halt the Germans near Montcornet and Serre. After an initial success against light vehicles, the French found themselves under steady attack by artillery, Stuka dive-bombers, and mechanized infantry. Towards the end of the day, de Gaulle withdrew to spare his remaining men.

De Gaulle gathered more tanks and made a new attack at Crecy on May 19th, 1940, but he again suffered a violent repulse. The 19th witnessed another disaster for the French when the highly capable General Henri Giraud fell prisoner to the Germans, prompting his 9th Army to desert en masse within hours. General Maurice Gamelin, the commander who oversaw the disastrous French defense up to that point, held a feast for his leading officers and then relinquished overall command to General Maxime Weygand.

On May 20th, just 11 days after the commencement of hostilities, leading elements of the 2nd Panzer Division under Rudolf Veiel reached the coast at the commune of Noyelles-sur-Mer, close to the mouth of the Somme River. Guderian's bold advance had cut off three French armies and the British Expeditionary Force (BEF) successfully in Belgium and the northeast corner of France.

May 21 was something of a respite for both sides, due mainly to the indecisiveness of the leaders of both the Allied and Axis forces. Guderian's and Rommel's panzer divisions held their line, reinforcing it with motorized infantry and artillery, while the OKW attempted to decide whether to strike north against the encircled French and British forces or south into France proper. Eventually, the OKW decided on a northward advance, but the order arrived in midafternoon and Guderian could do little more than prepare his forces for the following day's advance.

On May 22, Rommel attacked north towards Arras. A spoiling attack pinned him down for a while, but on the 23rd, he took the city and advanced past it. Guderian also sent a pair of panzer divisions north, aiming to seize Calais and Boulogne. Lord Gort and Maxime Weygand failed to meet and devise a plan, an event ascribed to the British commander's malice by the French but which actually resulted from appallingly bad communications.

Prime Minister Paul Reynaud announced the desperate situation to the French Senate in Paris that day, producing deep shock. Most government officials of France believed, up to that moment, in an imminent Allied victory. The Secretary of War, Marshal Petain – later head of the collaborationist Vichy government – argued for an armistice. Nevertheless, Weygand remained confident, albeit for reasons that might have been comical if not for the situation's deadly seriousness: "Despite his arduous experiences of the past twenty-four hours, the seventy-three-year-old Generalissimo arrived full of bounce and launched into his analysis of the situation on an evident note of optimism. 'So many mistakes have been made,' he began, 'that they give me confidence. I believe that in future we shall make less.'" (Horne, 2007, 389).

Weygand outlined a plan of bizarre optimism in which the entire trapped Allied force would turn south and "round up" the panzers in the course of one day. In the meantime, the Germans established numerous bridgeheads on the south bank of the Somme, to be used when the southward advance began. Panzers invested Boulogne on May 22nd, and on May 23rd, the British evacuated their troops at midnight. The French garrison surrendered at noon two days later on May 25th, recognizing their utterly hopeless position.

The initial investment of Calais fell to the 1st Panzer Division, but Guderian later ordered them onward to Dunkirk and replaced them with Ferdinand Schaal's 10th Panzer Division. On May 25th and 26th, the Germans attacked the city vigorously with tanks, artillery, infantry, and airstrikes by Junkers Ju 87 Stuka dive-bombers. Sir Winston Churchill and Sir Anthony Eden sent a message to the battered defenders, urging them to hold out as long as possible: "Defence of Calais to the utmost is of highest importance to our country as symbolising our continued co-operation with France. The eyes of the Empire are upon the defence of Calais, and H. M. Government are confident you and your gallant regiments will perform an exploit worthy of the British name." (Evans, 2000, 98).

Nevertheless, Schaal's fierce attacks overwhelmed the defenders. On May 27th, 47 men escaped in a yacht after hiding under a Nazi-held dock at the waterfront, but the other 3,000 British and 800 French soldiers in Calais surrendered to the Wehrmacht. With the Germans surging north all across Flanders, the British and French forces fell back towards Dunkirk, the last Channel port still in Allied possession, and the Germans closed in for the kill.

The British government ordered an evacuation of Dunkirk on May 26th, but the BEF and the French forces accompanying them could not escape that easily, however. Near catastrophe struck on May 28th when the Belgians surrendered to Germany, opening a colossal gap in the Allied lines. King Leopold III, showing consistency of character at least if not moral courage, informed the British and French of his planned capitulation only hours prior to the actual surrender, leaving them with practically no time to prepare for its disastrous military consequences. The action earned Leopold III such sobriquets as "King Rat" and "the Traitor King," nicknames he did little to disprove when he evinced more willingness to negotiate with Hitler for restoration of Belgian independence than he had shown in dealing with France and Britain, which sought to defend Belgium's freedom in the first place. British Prime Minister Sir Winston Churchill blasted the Belgian monarch's abrupt surrender in a detailed speech summarizing the repercussions: "The surrender of the Belgian Army compelled the British at the shortest notice to cover a flank to the sea more than 30 miles in length. Otherwise all would have been cut off, and all would have shared the fate to which King Leopold had condemned the finest army his country had ever formed. So in doing this and in exposing this flank, as anyone who followed the operations on the map will see, contact was lost between the British and two out of the three corps forming the First French Army." (Churchill, 2013, 174).

The BEF and their French allies in Dunkirk owed their escape to an unlikely source: the bombastic Luftwaffe leader, Hermann Goering. Goering wanted the glory of destroying the trapped allies for the Luftwaffe and persuaded Hitler to order the panzer divisions to halt. Without this error, the "Miracle of Dunkirk" – also known as "Operation Dynamo" – would likely have failed, and the Germans may have taken vast numbers of English and French prisoners, possibly ending British participation in the war.

Goering

Hitler, distracted by prospects of moving south through largely undefended French territory, realized too late that Goering's decision stemmed from emotion, not military logic. The British fought off the Luftwaffe, aided by foul weather which impeded the German pilots. The Channel port also lay within striking distance of airstrips in southern England, allowing British fighters to support the isolated troops.

Hitler eventually ordered Guderian into action again, and the heroism of the French 1ere Army helped save the situation for the Allied troops at Dunkirk. While the RAF flew 3,500 sorties to keep the Luftwaffe at bay, the First Army fought at Lille until May 31st against the full weight of 7 Wehrmacht divisions. Finally, the remaining 35,000 French soldiers, starving and without enough ammunition to continue fighting, surrendered.

Despite the escape of over 200,000 British soldiers at Dunkirk, Hitler and his generals still had reason to be pleased. The Germans now held 1,200,000 prisoners, large areas of northern France, all of Belgium and Low Countries, and could view the southern two-thirds of France as a juicy fruit ripe and ready to fall into their hands. With that, the OKW issued the order to move south from the Somme and complete the conquest of France on May 31st, 1940. The Germans mustered 143 divisions against the 60 divisions remaining to the French following the northern military catastrophe. The Germans gave this portion of their invasion the name "Fall Rot," or "Case Red" – the follow up to Fall Gelb, or "Case Yellow," the bold plan to take the north by encirclement.

Rommel led the drive south on June 5th. Other than a determined resistance from a small group of Colonial infantry holding Hengest, the Germans initially encountered only weak Allied resistance and pushed forward strongly, striking at any resistance with artillery or direct fire from the deadly Sturmgeschutz (StuG) III self-propelled guns, which proved excellent tank hunters later in the war.

Over the course of the next few days, the Germans continued to drive south across the open country between the Somme and the Seine. Isolated pockets of resistance, such as one at the small harbor of St. Valery en Caux, slowed their attack somewhat. For the most part, however, the Wehrmacht swept up the scattered French and British units they encountered as prisoners, sometimes immediately, at other times after a brief firefight, depending on the individual level of defiance found among the men of a particular unit.

On June 14, 1940, the Germans entered Paris without a fight. In fact, they arrived in the manner of a swarm of heavily-armed tourists, carrying cameras and taking each others' photographs while standing in front of various famous landmarks. The French government, of course, had declared loudly it would lead a memorable defense of the capital, only to flee four days before the first panzer-dust appeared on the northern horizon. The Germans, following them south, found enormous depots of unused weapons and ammunition, whole warehouses filled with tanks that never saw combat, and other mountains of supplies, many of which they appropriated for their own use.

A picture of German soldiers at the Arc de Triomphe

In all, the Germans lost some 160,000 men and 795 tanks in the fight for France. Panzer Is and IIs suffered badly, as did the backbone of the assault, the Panzer III. As in Poland, only the Panzer IV could be said to have performed consistently well on the battlefield. However, these losses were partially offset by the large number of captured French tanks. These tanks were used for reserve units and anti-partisan operations throughout the war. Some were sent to fight on the Eastern Front, where they were soon outclassed by Russian armor, but by this time, German industry was in high gear, and rolling out Panzer IIIs and IVs at a record rate and captured models weren't as necessary.

Some recent historians question whether the Third Reich intended to use Blitzkrieg tactics against France. According to the revisionist theories of these historians, the Wehrmacht anticipated a long, drawn-out war of attrition and the lightning-fast victory over the French resulted from serendipitous good fortune and French military weakness rather than deliberate German planning.

Though such questions cannot find a wholly conclusive answer now that all of the officers involved in the decision-making process are long dead, the course of the operations themselves offer significant clues to the actual German strategic intent. Taken with a final bit of objective evidence offered by Third Reich armament industry production figures, a fairly firm verdict becomes possible in this matter.

German production of weapons systems and supply of ammunition and fuel sufficed for a short war, not for a prolonged war of attrition. Hitler's delay in moving against the Soviet Union until well into 1941 highlights this fact; even the lightning campaign in France used enough resources to prompt a period of retrenchment and resupply before the next military adventure commenced. The Germans also used the same tactics and strategy as in Poland, a clear and well-documented instance of Blitzkrieg. Large-scale movements rather than slow, methodical advances provided the rule, while the Luftwaffe's Stuka dive-bombers furnished a lethal sledgehammer to break most local resistance and plunge onward deeper into enemy territory.

If anything, the OKW became frightened of their own success at one point and nearly aborted the Blitzkrieg at the time of Heinz Guderian's brief resignation. The fact that they nearly abandoned Blitzkrieg does not mean their original intention did not involve such a strategy, however. Gerd von Rundstedt's diplomatic solution and Guderian's creative use of insubordination restarted the juggernaut of Blitzkrieg and won an incredible victory for the Third Reich in just slightly more than a month.

Two other factors probably underlay the success of the Wehrmacht's "Lightning War" during the 1940 invasion of France. One involved the considerable incompetence of the French high command, especially their refusal to use their superior tanks in large, concentrated, active formations. This failed mentality was the product of ossified military thought coming from an older generation still fighting World War I in their own minds.

The other issue, the French's unwillingness to engage in another bloodbath even if it offered a chance of victory, sprang from a sort of national shock and mourning still remaining after World War I. The previous war decimated an entire generation of young Frenchmen, killing up to 38%

of certain age groups. Though France's soldiers often fought with outstanding valor in 1940, the French remained collectively war-weary from the horrors of World War I. Soldiers, generals, politicians, and ordinary people vividly recalled those lying in their hundreds of thousands in the graveyards of northern France and Belgium, and preferred a relatively mild defeat to burying another generation of young men.

The Early Stages of the North Africa Campaign

While Germany struggled and ultimately failed to knock the British out during the Battle of Britain, the Axis powers had to deal with the British in North Africa. An initial Italian thrust into British Egypt with the hopes of taking the Suez Canal proved disastrous; Operazione E, launched on September 13, 1940, soon ground to a halt only 105 km (65 miles) over the border, stopped by a mere British screening force and the Italians' own disorganization. Insufficient forces were ready for the vanguard and so the Italians stopped, fortified their positions, and waited for reinforcements.

The British counterattack was dubbed Operation Compass and began on December 9, 1940. Within days the Italians were in full retreat, only able to engage in disorganized rearguard actions. By the end of the counterthrust, which lasted until February 9, the British had advanced about a third of the way across Libya, taking the strategic port of Tobruk, killing or wounding about 16,000 Italians, taking 133,298 Italian and Libyan prisoners, and capturing or destroying 420 tanks, 845 guns, and 564 aircraft. The British lost only 1,900 men killed and wounded. The British only stopped their advance because many of their resources got diverted to the campaign in Greece and the harsh desert conditions had worn down their vehicles to the extent that a rest and refit were impossible to delay any further.

The main reason for this stunning reverse was the poor equipment of the Italian army. A shortage of trucks meant the bulk of the infantry had to march, so there could be no quick advance by the tankettes. They also had few anti-tank or anti-aircraft guns, and their armor was far inferior to that of the British. The Italians had a large number of L3/35 tankettes in their colony of Libya, but these proved easy prey to the British Matilda tank. There is some confusion with the name of this particular tank, as it is often used to refer to both the Mark I and Mark II, a completely different model.

An Italian L3/35 during the war

The Mark I was an Interwar period design that was far too slow, only traveling at 13 km/h (8 mph) and armed only with a machine gun. This reflected the old thinking of World War I that tanks should accompany infantry and take out machine gun nests and other pockets of resistance. The Mark I would have no chance of survival in the more modern war to come, and production only ran to 140 models before it was superseded by the Mark II. Both models fought with the BEF in the invasion of France, where the superiority of the Mark II over the Mark I was made clear.

The Mark II, popularly although not officially called Matilda, was one of the main tanks used by the British early in the war, and it was this model that crushed the Italian advance on Egypt. It measured 5.99 m x 2.60 m x 2.50 m (15.11 x 8.6 x 8.3 ft) and weighed 25 tons. It carried a 40 mm (1.57 in) gun and a machine gun, the model of which varied throughout the tank's long production. The main gun was derived from the Swedish Bofors model, one of the best guns of its time, and had a good penetration ability and good rate of fire. It carried only anti-tank rounds and no high explosives, its main purpose being to take out other tanks. The turret was cast as one piece, but unlike the French cast turrets, it was considerably larger and could house three men although in cramped conditions. The crew totaled four—a driver, gunner, loader, and commander. All but the driver were stationed in the turret.

Mark Pellegrini's picture of a Mark II

With a maximum armor thickness of 78 mm (3.07 inches), it was immune to most fire the Germans could bring against it, and the Italians could barely touch it at all. Although the side and back armor was thinner, 65-70 mm (2.56-2.76 in) thick, and 55 mm (2.17 in) respectively, it was still a well-protected vehicle from those angles as well. Even the top and bottom, difficult to hit in any circumstances, were protected with 20 mm (0.79 in) of armor. At the Battle of Arras during the invasion of France, Rommel was stopped short by a small number of Mark IIs until he trained the famous 88 mm (3.46 in) guns on them. These guns, initially meant as anti-aircraft pieces, proved their worth as artillery time and again throughout the war.

All this armor, of course, made it quite slow, only 26 km/h (16 mph) on the road and much slower on terrain. Thus it could be nothing more than an infantry tank. It had a range of 257 km (160 mi).

Nearly 3,000 units were produced, going through various engine improvements designated Mark III, Mark IV, and Mark V, the last being produced as late as 1943. The slow speed of this tank was never improved and it found itself literally losing the race to better models.

In Operation Compass, the British also fielded a large number of faster Cruiser tanks. These sacrificed some armor in exchange for speed and maneuverability, and they were similar to the French "cavalry" tanks in that they were designed to take advantage of breaks in the enemy line to make rapid thrusts into rear areas. They were also good for flanking maneuvers and quick advances as the vanguard of a motorized force. Several versions of these cruisers were produced in the Interwar period but the most numerous and long lasting was the Mark IV.

The Mark IV A13 measured 6 m x 2.54 m x 2.59 m (19.9 x 8.4 x 8.6 ft), weighed 14.75 long tons (16.52 regular tons), had a top speed of 48 km/h (30 mph), and a range of 140 km (90 mi). The crew of four (driver, gunner, loader, commander) served a QF Vickers 2-pdr (40 mm/1.57 in) gun and a coaxial 0.303 (7.7 mm) Vickers machine gun. The British used the "pound" system of gun designation dating back to before the Napoleonic era, but this designation often had little to do with the actual weight of the round. This gun performed well against the lighter Italian tanks and Panzer Is and IIs. Armor ranged from 25 mm (1 in) to just 6 mm (.23 in), thus is was vulnerable to the Panzer III and IV as well as German anti-tank guns. It did well enough in the field that 890 were produced, more than twice as many as all three earlier models combined.

The earlier Marks I-III all saw service in France and North Africa, but they had many problems, such as insufficient armor and poor suspension systems. By 1941, those few that hadn't been knocked out or captured were reserved as training vehicles. The Mark IV endured, its design sturdy enough to be reliable even in the harsh conditions of the North African desert.

Besides the tankettes, the Italians had 72 of the new Fiat M11/39 tanks. This was the first Italian medium tank. It was unusual in that it had twin 8 mm (.31 in) machine guns on its turret and the main 37 mm (1.46 in) gun on the front of the hull. This was due to the design not being robust enough to deal with even such a modestly sized gun in the turret. The gun was placed on the right side of the hull where the gunner sat, while the driver sat on the left. Its traverse was limited to only 15° on each side. The commander sat in the turret, and was also responsible for the machine guns and the radio, making him as overworked as his French counterparts.

Fiat M11/39 tanks during the war

The M11/39 measured 4.7 m x 2.2 m x 2.3 m (15.42 x 7.22 x 7.55 ft), weighed 11.2 tons, had a speed of 32.2 km/h (20 mph), and a range of 200 km (125 mi). The armor ranged from 6 to 30 mm (0.24-1.18 in). This was fairly weak for the time, and was weakened further by being assembled by bolting the plates onto the chassis rather than casting or welding them. The British found that the 2-pounder guns (40 mm/1.57 in) given to their tanks and infantry units could pierce it with ease.

So the Italians had gotten it half right. They had created a vehicle with a good speed and range and a decently powerful gun, but with weak armor and a ridiculous weapons configuration that almost guaranteed its destruction when facing fully modern British tanks. In the end, only a hundred of these models were produced, starting in April of 1939 and ending in mid-1940.

The M11/39 was still understrength compared to what it had to face in North Africa. They were quickly wiped out in Operation Compass although a few fought on in places like the Italian Somaliland for a time, but meanwhile the Italians rushed to produce a stronger tank and brought out the Fiat M13/40. This was considerably more robust, with improved armor and a 47 mm (1.85 in) main gun that was finally positioned in the turret. Italy had its first proper tank.

The M13/40 reused the M1/39 hull with reinforced suspension to deal with the increased weight of the improved armor. Thus it measured 4.7 m x 2.2 m x 2.3 m (15.42 x 7.22 x 7.55 ft), weighed of 13 tons, had a speed of 32 km/h (20 mph), and a range of 200 km (120 mi). Armor ranged in thickness from 25 to 42 mm (0.98-1.65 in) but like its predecessor was bolted on, so every impact ran the chance of a bolt or spall flying around the inside. Of the four crewmen, the commander and loader sat in the turret while the driver and machine gunner/radio operator sat in the hull. Some but not all units were fitted with a radio.

Besides the main gun, the turret was also supplied with a coaxial 8 mm (0.31 in) machine gun, and the hull had twin 8 mm (0.31 in) machine guns.

The M13/40 performed well, its gun having good armor piercing capabilities, able to pierce 45 mm (2.16 in) at 500 m (550 yards). Almost 800 models were produced from 1940 to 1942 until it was gradually replaced by the M14/41.

The first 37 of these tanks made it to Libya in early October, followed by 46 more on 12 December. Those in the first two shipments made it in time to fight in Operation Compass. Although they performed well, they were too few in number to stem the tide and many were captured, most notably by the Australians who reused them after painting large kangaroos on their sides.

By the time further shipments arrived, Operation Compass had already achieved its stunning victory. The war in North Africa, however, was far from over.

As happened throughout the war, the Germans had to come in and save their Italian allies. The Desert Fox, Erwin Rommel, was sent with what would become the legendary Afrika Corps. The first units arrived on February 14, 1941, during a lull in the fighting while the British rested, refitted, and consolidated their gains. The Italians were prostrate, with the entire Tenth Army gone, and they had no strength to carry out any sort of offensive on their own. They still had a large number of men and an increasing number of tanks in the region, however, and would play an active role in the campaigns to come.

Rommel

The bulk of the fighting would be taken care of by the Germans. For his armored divisions, Rommel received a number of Panzer Is and IIs. While outgunned by the British, the open landscape proved advantageous to the fast little vehicles and Rommel continued to use them throughout the campaign. The backbone of his campaign, however, were later model Panzer IIIs that had better firepower and armor than the troublesome earlier models of the Polish and French campaigns. He received a few dozen Panzer IVs, and while these proved effective against British and later American armor, they were too outnumbered to turn the tide in Rommel's favor in the end.

However, in the early stages of the North African campaigns, Rommel did quite well. He quickly saw that most of his armor couldn't stand up to the Matilda, so he became adept at outflanking the slow-moving tank and bringing to bear his artillery and AA guns. Lighter guns such as the PaK 36 and 41 proved incapable of piercing the Matilda's armor, so he favored his 88 mm AA guns. While the Matilda's light gun did well against the Panzer I and II, it had trouble piercing the thicker armor of the Panzer III and IV. The British also allowed themselves to be lured into countless ambushes by the fast-moving and clever commander.

The Matilda proved itself poorly suited for desert warfare. Its engine had a tendency to overheat and drivers had trouble steering through sand. Thus, starting in late 1941, the Matilda was gradually replaced by the new Valentine tank. Using the A9-A10 Cruiser chassis, it had a lower, more compact turret and slightly thinner armor although better than most other tanks of its day. It measured 5.41 m x 2.62 m x 2.27 m (7.9 x 8.7 x 7.5 ft), weighed 16 long tons (17.9 tons), a speed of 24 km/h (15 mph), a range of 140 km (90 mi), and armor ranging from 8 to 65 mm (0.31 to 2.56 in).

The turret had a 2 pdr (40 mm/1.57 in) gun and a 7.62 mm (0.3 in) machine gun. The turret had room for only two men, the gunner and the commander while the driver sat in the hull. The commander was overworked by also acting as machine gunner, radio operator, and loader for the main gun.

While it was undergunned and cramped, it performed remarkably well in desert conditions and its low profile made it harder to hit. The design proved so successful and enduring that some 8,300 units were produced in 18 versions throughout the war, including Canadian and U.S. versions. The statistics given above are for the Mark II, the first large-scale production (700 units as opposed to 350 for the Mark I) and the one that saw the most fighting in North Africa in 1941.

Rommel had more problems than the British tanks. The standard British field gun, the 6-pounder (57 mm/2.24 in), had an armor piercing shell that could penetrate 68 mm of armor at 1,000 yards (914.4 m). This accurate and quick-firing weapon proved the bane of Panzer crews. In addition, Rommel was frustrated throughout the campaign by an overstretched and uncertain supply line that led to constant shortages of pretty much everything. While German U-boats are given a large amount of coverage in World War II literature, the British had submarines too, and they proved highly effective, along with sea and air forces, in destroying supply convoys headed to Axis-held areas of North Africa.

In addition, Rommel had to face superior Allied air power, which destroyed his land convoys, blew up bridges along his supply routes, and knocked out tanks before they even got into battle. The Germans also discovered that while their tank tactics proved effective when they enjoyed the element of surprise against an inferior foe, they did not do so well amidst the vast distances of North Africa against a foe that had excellent aerial reconnaissance.

The Eastern Front

By far the biggest operation of the war was the German invasion of the Soviet Union, an invasion on a vast scale with the aim of taking the agricultural land of western Russia and the Ukraine, the oil fields of the Ukraine, and the capital of Moscow. Launched on June 22, 1941, it was the biggest invasion in history, involving 3.8 million Germans and some 3,500 tanks.

Many older model tanks and captured tanks found their way into this campaign, but were quickly scrapped when they came up against superior Soviet armor. The 152 Panzer Is that took part in the opening weeks of the campaign suffered badly and were soon placed in the rear area for police duties in occupied areas. The 743 Panzer IIs were relegated to a scouting role and had to be fitted with extra armor plates to have any hope of survival. Even so, many were lost and the remainder were used for support roles or given to allies such as Slovakia and Bulgaria. Thus, the 972 Panzer IIIs and 417 Panzer IVs had to bear the brunt of the fighting.

The Germans faced a tough foe, as Russian tanks outnumbered German tanks 4-1. Most were light, fast models such as the T-26 mentioned above and the BT-7. This model followed up on the Interwar B2 and B-5 models, both of which were obsolete when the war began. All three were designed as cavalry tanks.

The BT-7 measured 5.66 m x 2.41 m x 2.29 m (18.57 x 7.91 x 7.51 ft), weighed 13.8 tons, could run an impressive 86 km/h (53 mph) with a range of 200 km (120 mi), and had 6 to 22 mm (0.24-0.87 in) of armor. Its crew of three (driver, gunner, commander/loader) manned a 45 mm (1.77 in) main gun and coaxial 7.62 mm (0.3 in) machine gun. Later versions had additional machine guns on the rear of the turret as well as on the top of the turret, this last one manned by someone first opening the hatch. Top-mounted machine guns became common later in the war as an anti-aircraft measure.

Nearly 5,000 BT-7s were produced, the main series being launched in 1937 and the last series in 1940, at which point it was already being outpaced by more modern designs. The BT-7 was a vital stopgap to resist Operation Barbarossa, and it paid a heavy price. In the first year of the campaign, some 2,000 BT-7s were lost due to enemy action or breakdowns.

The Soviets were also beginning to field more serious tanks, the T-34 and the KV-1. Both were in small numbers in the early stages of the campaign, but Soviet industry performed miracles and as the months wore on, the Germans found themselves facing more and more of these tough models.

The T-34 has sometimes been called the tank that won World War II. It became the backbone of the Soviet armored divisions, and provided a good balance between speed, armor, and firepower. While not free of engineering glitches, it was able to withstand the Russian winter much better than its opponents.

The production history of this model is complex, with factories often producing slightly different models simultaneously. Plus there were many modifications during its long production run. The model 1940 was the first mass production model, but the model 1941 was a significant improvement and more popular so its statistics are what we give here. It measured 5.92 m x 3 m x 2.4 m (19.42 x 9.84 x 7.87 ft), weighed 28.1 tons, had a speed of 55 km/h (34 mph), and a range of 300 km (186 mi).

The main gun was a powerful 76.2 mm (3 in) piece. Many historians refer to the early T-34s as the T-34/76 to differentiate it from the upgunned T-34/85 that began production in 1943 and appeared on the front in significant numbers the following year. It had a 7.62 mm (0.3 in) machine gun in the turret, another in the hull, and a third stowed. Later models had one on the top as anti-aircraft protection.

The armor was steeply sloped and proved impervious to pretty much everything the Germans could throw at it in 1941 except for the 88 mm guns. For smaller pieces like those on the Panzer IV, the only hope was to hit a T-34's tracks and disable it. The later Panzer V (aka Panther) was a direct response to this threat.

The Soviet medium and heavy tanks differed from those of other nations in that they had a more uniform armor thickness. The T-34 had up to 45 mm (1.77 in) on the front of the hull, 40 mm (1.57 in) on the sides and rear, 20 mm/16 mm (0.79/0.63 in) on the hull top/bottom, and 45 or 52 mm (1.77 or 2.03 in) on the turret. Thus, when the Germans outflanked the T-34 looking to hit a weak spot, they got a nasty surprise.

All units were supplied with a radio, thereby negating yet another German advantage.

In all, more than 35,000 T-34s were produced during the war, quickly usurping all production of the T-26 and BT-7. It became an icon of the Soviet armed forces.

The KV-1 was an even heavier tank that first saw production in 1939, although the Soviets fielded them in insufficient numbers in 1941. It measured 5.8 m x 4.2 m x 2.32 m (19.02 × 13.78 × 7.61 ft). It weighed a hefty 45 tons but could achieve a decent top speed of 38 km/h (26 mph) with a range of 200 km (140 mi). Its four-man crew (driver, two gunners, and a commander) manned a 76.2 mm (3 in) main gun and three 7.62 mm (0.3 in) machine guns—one coaxial with the main gun, one on the rear of the turret, and one on the front of the hull. Armor was 75 mm (2.95 in) on the front and sides, 70 mm (2.76 in) on the rear, and 30 mm (1.18 in) on the top and bottom. There were several variations of the KV-1, with some having up to 110-120 mm (4.33-4.72 in) in armor. Also, later models had cast turrets instead of welded turrets, adding additional strength.

The KV-1

More than 5,000 KV-1s were produced during the war, but it was eventually superseded by the T-34. The KV-1 had the same gun as the T-34, but was much slower and considerably more expensive. Thus the T-34 was the better all-around tank.

While the first few months of Operation Barbarossa were a smashing success that drove the Soviets back hundreds of miles and inflicted heavy casualties, the Germans did not have it all their own way. Commanders made numerous mistakes due to the overconfidence instilled in them from the Polish and French campaigns, as well as the rapid advance in those heady first few weeks across the Russian steppes.

One general who found himself dealing with a sharp learning curve was Erich von Manstein. Leading the 8th Panzer Division, the 3rd Infantry Division (motorized), and the 290th Infantry Division, he was part of a drive across the Baltic states with the objective of taking the city of Soltsy and crossing the Luga River, thus leaving the way open to the key port of Leningrad 200 km (120 miles) to the north which would be the final objective.

Manstein

Manstein attacked across the Nieman River on June 22, and at first all went well, with Manstein driving his Panzers hard and brushing aside the surprised and weak resistance. He easily crossed the river and advanced 70 km (44 miles) on the first day. His advance was so rapid that he was able to take the bridges across his next major barrier, the Dvina River, intact.

It was there that he ran into problems. His column was strung out with the rest of Heeresgruppe Nord under General Reinhardt 100 km (62 miles) behind him on his right, thus leaving his right flank wide open. His one non-motorized infantry division was practically running all day to keep up, and his motorized divisions had almost run out of fuel and were not getting supplies quickly enough from the rear areas.

The Soviets sensed weakness and decided to push Manstein back over the Dvina River. As Soviet tactical bombers pummeled his bridgeheads, the Soviet 21st Mechanical Corps under Major-General Dmitri Lelyushenko hit the bridgeheads with 60 BT-7 light tanks. Manstein kept his head and managed to hold the bridgeheads, destroying most of the BT-7s, but he was unable to follow up his victory with a counterattack for lack of fuel.

After a few days, Reinhardt's units on his right flank caught up and Manstein got his fuel, at which point they continued their drive towards Leningrad. Added to Manstein's corps was the motorized SS Division *Totenkopf* ("Death's Head"). Once again Manstein and Reinhardt advanced rapidly and once again their corps became separated. In Poland and France, their enemies had not had the mobility or sufficient armor to take advantage of such an opportunity, but the Soviets were opponents of a higher order. On July 15, with Manstein's divisions strung out along the road with little flank protection from Reinhardt, who had veered to the east, the Soviet 11th Army under Major-General Ivan Lazarev launched a pincer attack with a tank division consisting of more than 100 T-26 tanks, a full rifle division, and three understrength rifle divisions. They succeeded in cutting the main road behind Manstein and inflicting heavy losses all along his column.

Lazarev

The lead division, the 8th Panzer Division, got completely cut off. It took two days for them to fight out of the encirclement, and they sustained such heavy losses that they had to go to the rear for rest and refitting. The Battle of Soltsy had been a major defeat, slowing the advance on Leningrad.

Manstein later learned another lesson in the Crimea while besieging Sevastopol. The Russian defenders actually outnumbered Manstein's forces and launched three counterattacks against him, all of which he repulsed, but then Manstein blundered by sending the 22nd Panzer Division on a counterattack into Soviet defenses. Without the support of infantry or artillery, or even pioneers to clear the way, he ordered the Panzers into an area of minefields and anti-tank ditches. The result was a debacle, and Manstein learned that unlike in Poland and France, one could not send tanks unsupported against the Soviets.

These examples may suggest Manstein was a poor commander, but nothing could be further from the truth. Tank warfare was new to everyone at this point, and even the greatest leaders had a lot to learn. Manstein soon discovered how to use his tank divisions to their best advantage, and after the Crimea he always made sure to support them as well as he could with his often limited resources.

A more typical engagement, one that demonstrated the strengths and weaknesses of both sides, was the Battle of Dubno-Brody, which took place from June 23-30, 1941 in the Ukraine. Little is written on this major engagement in English, and hard figures are somewhat difficult to track down, but if the upper estimates of the tank numbers involved are correct, it was a bigger battle than Kursk in 1943, the battle that has gone down in history as the largest tank battle in history. Of course, the winners write the history, and Kursk was a Soviet victory, whereas the battle of Dubno-Brody was not, which may explain why it has been underplayed.

A Panzer III tank at the start of the campaign

The Soviets had eight tank divisions concentrated in four corps with a total of 2,418 tanks, of which 312 were T-34s and KV-1s. Virtually all of these superior tanks were in the 8th and 15th Mechanized Corps, the 9th Corps having no T-34s or KV-1s and the 19th having only five. The rest of the tanks were lighter, earlier models like the T-26 and BT-7. Thus, only 13% of their tanks were truly effective, and that would have a telling outcome on the battle.

A picture of German soldiers inspecting a disabled BT-7

On the German side there were four tank divisions in two tank corps. The 3rd Panzer Corps had 296 tanks, of which 140 were Panzer IIIs and IVs, while the 48th Panzer Corps had 289 tanks, or which 135 were Panzer IIIs and IVs. Thus out of a total of 585 tanks, only 47% were late models, the rest being Panzer Is and IIs and a few captured models.

Thus, while the Soviet tanks outnumbered the Panzers more than four to one, the Soviets enjoyed only a slight edge in terms of modern tanks.

The Germans were driving for Kiev, and the Soviet generals had been given orders straight from Stalin to launch counterattacks against the German advance to knock it off balance. The Russian forces on the ground were in no condition to do this, but an order from Stalin could not be disobeyed. Poor preparation, poor transport, and a long travel distance meant the Soviet units got to their launch points late and strung out. Transport was so bad that many artillery pieces simply got left behind. Mechanical failures and persistent Luftwaffe bombing—the Germans enjoying near-total dominance of the skies—whittled down the vehicle numbers. Conflicting orders from various command centers also added to the confusion.

The two armies finally clashed on June 26. The Germans had already taken the city of Dubno on the Ikva River, held by the 11th Panzer Division. To its north were the 13th and 14th divisions, behind a bend in the river that put them well behind (to the northwest of) the 11th. Behind the 11th, to the west and a little south, was the 16th Panzer division. Thus the 11th, while having taken the important city, was in a perilous salient the Soviets hoped to cut off. The 19th Soviet Mechanized Corps, with virtually no modern tanks, hit the 11th Panzer directly on its front, while the 9th, with no modern tanks, hit the 13th and 14th Panzer to the north. The 8th Soviet Mechanized Corps, strong in modern tanks, came up from the south, passing the city of Brody to hit the 16th Panzer.

The 13th and 14th Panzer ground down the more numerous 9th Soviet and started to push them back. The 11th Panzer also gained ground against a larger but less modern foe.

To the south the Germans didn't do as well. The 16th Panzer division had to withdraw in the face of superior T-34s and KV-1s. This left the right flank of the 11th wide open. To the southeast was the Soviet 37th Infantry Corps which could have exploited this gap but for reasons that have never been made clear, but probably have something to do with the confusion at the Soviet high command, sat out the entire battle.

Similarly, the 15th Mechanized Corps passed by to the west of the battle, being sent the completely wrong direction by the high command. Their numerous modern tanks would not be used in the fight.

Realizing they were on their own, the 8th Mechanized Corps split itself, sending part of its strength to hit the 11th Panzer in the rear, ejecting its rearguard out of Dubno.

On June 28, suffering heavy losses, the 9th Soviet Mechanized Corps retreated, and the 13th and 14th Panzer followed, passing beyond reach of the rest of the fighting. Now the 11th Panzer was totally cut off, and yet the 8th Mechanized Corps did not press its advantage, instead basing itself in Dubno and awaiting reinforcements. At this point salvation came in the form of the German 29th Infantry, who have been quick marching to get to the battlefield. It hit the 8th Mechanized Corps from the northeast and north, putting the Russians on the defensive. Now the 8th found itself nearly surrounded and had to flee south.

Poor command structure and total disorganization turned what could have been a solid victory into a major defeat. The Soviets lost more than 90% of their tanks, many due to mechanical failure. The Germans, too, suffered heavily, losing about 70% of their armor. These losses were mostly due to the 8th Mechanized Corps, the one modern corps the Soviets brought to the battle. One wonders what would have happened if the 15th Mechanized Corps with its T-34s and KV-1s would have done if they had attacked from the German rear like they could have.

While the campaign in France in 1940 had signaled to the more perceptive officers in the German command that they needed more robust tanks, the invasion of Russia the following year was the real wakeup call. It was there the Panzers faced large numbers of superior tanks for the first time. Tanks such as the T-34 and the KV-1 were all but impervious to German field guns and the Panzer IV, while their powerful main guns were capable of knocking out the strongest of German armor.

Another major advantage of Soviet armor was that the units ran on diesel, meaning the engines were less likely to freeze up in the winter and were easier to start. The Germans, on the other hand, ran on regular gasoline and had constant trouble with the sub-zero temperatures of the Russian winter.

While the Germans never switched to diesel, they did hasten to create more powerful tanks. The first of these was the Panzer V, the so-called Panther tank. A major improvement on the Panzer IV, the first units rolled off the assembly line in 1942, and more than 6,000 units were built before the end of the war, making it the third most-produced German armored fighting vehicle of the war after the StuG III assault gun and the Panzer IV.

The Panther went through many redesigns, the most popular being the Ausf. G (*Ausführung G* or "Model G"), produced from the beginning of March 1944 and lasting through the end of the war. A total of about 3,000 units of this model were produced. It measured 8.66 x 3.27 x 2.99 m (28.41 x 10.73 x 9.81 ft), weighed 44.8 tons, had a speed of 48 km/h (29 mph), and a range of 250 km (160 mi). The five-man crew (commander, gunner, loader, driver, and radioman/machine gunner) was protected by up to 80 mm (3.15 in) of armor, but the steep slope made it equivalent to 120 mm (4.72 in), and the bottom and top were rather vulnerable, having only 10 mm (0.39 in) of armor. The wheels were interleaved to reduce ground pressure from the heavy vehicle and to protect the lower hull, meaning that a hit by an anti-tank gun might only disable the vehicle and spare the crew. The main gun was a powerful, long-barreled 75 mm (2.95 in) gun alongside two 7.9 mm (0.31 in) machine guns—one of them coaxial, the other on the front of the hull along with the main gun—a standard arrangement for most tanks in the middle and late war period.

The Panther introduced a number of technological innovations. Some—like the automatic fire extinguisher—suffered from malfunctions while others—like the infrared searchlight and scope for night fighting—were well ahead of their time.

Germany developed night-vision devices as early as 1939. The first was a prototype for use with the 37 mm PaK 35/36 anti-tank gun. Actual field use didn't commence until an improved version of the 75 mm PaK 40 anti-tank gun and the Marder II self-propelled anti-tank gun were introduced in 1942. The Panther's infrared searchlight had a range of 600 m (1,969 ft). While it was a great advance in technology, the infrared sensors underwent a long testing phase, though it appears only 50 Panthers had ever been outfitted with them. They only began to see combat in March of 1945, too late to affect the outcome of the war. Even so, in April of 1945, a group of Panthers using infrared sensors wiped out an entire platoon of British tanks.

The Panther was not the perfect tank. Early models had various mechanical problems, and the unit price was high. Despite the thick armor, the Panther was still vulnerable to side hits from heavy guns such as the British 17-pdr (76.2 mm/3 in), and heavier tanks such as the Russian IS-2. Also, the turret had a fairly slow traverse speed—only 10 degrees per second, half the traverse speed of the American Sherman tank—and even a second delayed reaction time could prove fatal in battle. Also, the interleaved wheels were more liable to clog with snow and mud, the two banes of every tanker's existence on the Eastern Front. Its long barrel and sizeable width hampered it when it had to fight in urban situations and the hedgerows of Normandy.

The first early model Panthers saw service in Operation Citadel (*Unternehmen Zitadelle*), the Germans' main offensive on the Eastern Front in the summer of 1943, hoping to get rid of the Soviet salient around Kursk. This led to what is touted as the largest tank battle of all time, although as we saw in the first part of this series, the 1941 Battle of Dubno-Brody may have been larger. While the Panthers made up only seven percent of the total number of tanks in Operation Citadel and the early models were plagued with mechanical problems, they still accounted for an impressive 267 kills, proving them superior to any Soviet tank. By the beginning of the following year, most of the early mechanical issues had been ironed out, and the Panzer V truly came into its own.

The Panther was considered a medium tank. The Germans were also producing heavy tanks in the form of the Panzer VI, more popularly known as the Tiger. This tank in its Ausf. E configuration measured 8.45 m x 3.70 m x 3.00 m (27.72 x 12.14 x 9.84 ft), weighed 56.9 tons, could go up to 45 km/h (28 mph), and had a range of 125 km (78 miles). Its crew of five (commander, driver, gunner, loader, and radio operator/machine gunner) were protected by 100 mm (3.94 in) of armor in the front, 80 mm (3.15 in) on the sides and rear, and 25 mm (1 in) on the top and bottom. They had an 88 mm (3.4 in) main gun and two 7.92 mm (0.31 in) machine guns, one coaxial and the other on the front hull. Like the Panther, it had interleaved wheels.

While it had been a longtime dream to get the famous 88 mm gun onto a tank, the Panther's gun was more effective as a tank buster, but the Tiger's overall design superiority made it the most feared German tank among the Allies. Its hefty price tag—it cost more than four StuG IIIs—and late incorporation meant that only 1,346 were ever built. Despite its small numbers, it took out a disproportionate number of Allied tanks and became an icon of German power and engineering.

The planning phase for the Tiger started in late 1935 as an answer to the heavy French tanks, but it wasn't until 1942 that the first models rolled off the assembly line. The sides had 60 mm (2.36 in) armored shields that could be lowered to protect the tracks. This type of side armor had already been used on an ad hoc basis for several tanks, thanks to the Allied habit of targeting the tracks, often the only part of the more advanced Panzers their guns were able to affect. Because the Tiger was too heavy for most bridges, it was made watertight and given a sealable air intake system so it could ford rivers.

There was also a focus on training the crews—only the most elite tankers had the honor of being in the crew of a Tiger.

Because of the cost and the small number produced, the Tigers tended to work in small-unit operations in tandem with groups of Panzer IIIs to do the lighter work as they took out tough pockets of resistance or broke through enemy lines. Early models first saw action in the summer of 1942 but had to be recalled to work out their mechanical issues. Later models were delivered in monthly batches in early 1943, and this is when their true operational history began. The last delivery was in August 1944, after which the Tiger was replaced by the Tiger II.

Otto Carius, who had commanded a Tiger on the Eastern Front, recalled the model with joy. He had been assigned to a Tiger unit in early 1943, and said of the new tank, "It really drove just like a car. With two fingers, we could literally shift 700 horsepower, steer 60 tons, drive 45 kilometers an hour on roads, and trek 20 kilometers an hour cross-country. In consideration of the equipment, however, we only drove twenty to twenty-five kilometers on the roads and correspondingly slower cross-country."

Carius had first joined the opening push of Operation Barbarossa in a Panzer 38(t), a Czech model brought into German service, which was soon knocked out by a Russian 47 mm gun, and Otto was wounded; he liked the Tiger much better.

The commander recalled how each position in the tank had its own special kind of stress. The loader was in what was perhaps the worst position, because while his was the least skilled job, he couldn't see out, and the suspense could become almost unbearable. The driver had to have a skilled touch and a sense of the terrain, but once the tank was in position, he had to sit idle and alert as the rest of the crew slugged it out with the enemy.

Carius also remembers the Tiger's main foe: "The T34, with its good armor, ideal shape, and magnificent 76.2 mm long-barreled cannon was universally feared and a threat to every German tank up to the end of the war. What were we supposed to do with these monstrosities that were being committed in quantity against us? We could only 'knock at the door' with our cannons;

inside, the Russians were able to play an undisturbed hand of cards. At that time [the opening phase of Operation Barbarossa], the 37 mm PaK was still our strongest armor-defeating weapon. If lucky, we could hit the T34 on the turret ring and jam it. With a whole lot more luck, it became combat ineffective. Certainly not a very positive situation! Our only salvation was the 88 mm flak. Even this new Russian tank could be effectively engaged with it. We started paying the utmost respect to the flak troops who previously had sometimes received a condescending smile from us."

The Tiger is perhaps unique in World War II in that waiting for its delivery delayed a major offensive. The German defeat at Stalingrad in February of 1943 had severely demoralized the Wehrmacht and shaken Hitler, who was determined to get back on the front foot in the coming spring and hence planned Operation Citadel. Its objective was to get rid of the salient sticking into the German lines around the railway hub of Kursk. The Germans decided to attack in a pincer movement against the salient's northern and southern flanks in order rid them of the salient, shortening their lines and trapping the Soviet forces.

Originally planned for May, Operation Citadel was put off until July so that sufficient numbers of new tanks, especially the Tiger, could make it to the front. Naturally, this massive buildup did not go unnoticed; helped by British intelligence, the Soviets were able to pinpoint the exact date and location of the offensive. The Soviets laid mines and artillery kill zones and established camouflaged strong points along eight defensive lines, 250 km (150 mi) deep.

Russian Commander Georgy Zhukov wrote to Stalin, "I consider it inadvisable for our forces to go over to the offensive in the very first days of the campaign in order to forestall the enemy. It would be better to make the enemy exhaust himself against our defenses, and knock out his tanks and then, bringing up fresh reserves, to go over to the general offensive which would finally finish off his main force."

To do this, the Soviets had assembled 1.3 million men, 3,600 tanks, 20,000 guns and mortars, and 2,800 aircraft. Their defensive lines included 504,000 anti-tank mines and 440,000 anti-personnel mines, plus thousands of miles of trenches. The Germans brought to bear 900,000 troops, 3,250 tanks and mobile assault guns, including 270 Tigers and 2,100 aircraft.

The launch date was set for July 5, but the Soviets preempted the Germans by starting a massive artillery bombardment at 2:00 a.m. that morning, thereby signaling they were aware of German plans. After some initial confusion, the Germans set out with their heavy tanks in the lead, the medium tanks coming up behind, and the infantry behind them. They got bogged down in the minefields and provided cover fire for the engineering units trying to clear a path, but in the process, the Germans took heavy casualties. Even the Tigers began to fall prey to Soviet guns once the Russians had discovered their armor was thinner on the sides and hit them with crossfire.

The famed tank battle started on the 7th with an estimated 6,000 tanks in the field, making it arguably the largest tank battle in history. Aircraft played an important role in this fight. At first, the Luftwaffe and Soviet Air Force were evenly matched, but after long hours of bitter fighting, the Luftwaffe got the upper hand and began to dominate the skies. Using dive bombers to hit the Soviet armor, the Luftwaffe was solely responsible for stopping the huge Soviet counterattack, the first time air power had halted a major advance by an armored column. Soviet planes also took out German armor, but not nearly as efficiently.

In the end, it was the superior numbers and firepower of the Soviet armor that won the day. The Germans lost some 184,000 killed or wounded, as well as 760 tanks and 661 aircraft. From then on, the strategic initiative on the Eastern Front would belong to the Soviets.

Allied Tanks in North Africa and Western Europe

1942 saw the Allies pushing back against the Axis powers, and it was the year the war in Europe and North Africa hung in the balance. Only in retrospect was it clear that 1942 was the year the Allies began to turn the tide.

At the time, the United Kingdom and Commonwealth countries were still fielding inferior tanks to the Panzers. They were mainly using the slow-moving but powerful Matilda and the quick but under-armored and under-gunned Cruiser IV. The new Valentine Tank, introduced in 1941, was a compromise between the two models, and though it was highly successful, the British were not done designing tanks yet.

The Churchill tank used a design that was even more robust. It appeared in battle in mid-1942 and performed excellently in the open terrain of North Africa. The design went through many iterations and variants, the most popular being the A22F Mark VII, which first saw combat in 1944. This version measured 7.44 x 3.25 x 2.49 m (24.41 x 10.66 x 8.17 ft) and weighed 40 tons. It was slow, with a top speed of only 24 km/h (15 mph) and a range of 90 km (56 mi), but this was compensated with heavy armor and an effective gun. The five-man crew (commander, driver, co-driver/hull gunner, main gunner, and loader/radio operator) manned a 75 mm (2.95 in) main gun and two 0.303 (7.7 mm) machine guns, one coaxial and one on the front hull. Armor ranged from 25 to 152 mm (0.98-5.98 in). Although the armor was almost vertical—thus losing the advantage of sloping—it remained an incredibly tough design. During the Second Battle of El Alamein in late 1942, one Churchill took 80 hits but none of them penetrated, and the crew lived to see another day, although perhaps with a ringing in their ears from all of the impacts.

The Churchill tank Mark IV

Earlier versions had weaker guns and mechanical issues. Both of these problems were solved with later productions, but even with the 75 mm main gun, the Churchill had difficulty facing the Panther and the Tiger.

The Churchill proved to be one of the toughest, most reliable tanks fielded by the British. It could go long distances before needing servicing, could withstand all but the most powerful guns and was capable of ascending inclines impassible to all other Allied tanks. This proved especially important in Tunisia's rough, mountainous terrain. They also saw extensive use in Italy for the same reason. The Churchill was modified for many tasks including being fitted with a howitzer, a flamethrower, a heavy mortar to destroy bunkers, and a spinning flail of chains to take out mines. A total of 7,368 units were produced, a testament to its usefulness. A shipment of 301 Mark III and IV Churchills even made it to Russia as part of the Lend-Lease Program, where they participated in the Battle of Kursk.

The Churchill was the last British infantry tank. Good for slow-moving slugfests and supporting foot soldiers, it could not keep up with quick armored thrusts. Innovations continued with the Cruiser series, culminating in the Cruiser VI "Crusader."

The Crusader came in three varieties: the Marks I, II, and III. All were the same except for armament and crew. They measured 5.97 x 2.77 x 2.24 m (19.6 x 9.1 x 7.35 ft) and ranged from 18.8 to 19.7 tons. They had a top speed of 42 km/h (26 mph) and a range of 322 km (146 mi).

The Mark I and II had the old, 2pdr (40 mm/1.57 in) main gun, far too undersized to deal with later model Panzers. The Mark II was up-gunned to a 6pdr (57 mm/2.24 in), the standard infantry artillery piece that performed well against tanks and was produced in mass quantities. Secondary armament came in the form of one or two 7.9 mm (0.303 in) machine guns. Only the Mark I had two machine guns, the second in an awkward, miniature turret in front of the main one. This was later done away with, and only the coaxial machine gun was kept. Maximum armor thickness was consistently upgraded in each of the versions from 40 to 49 to 51 mm (1.57 to 1.93 to 2 in).

A Crusader tank in North Africa

Already in the testing phase in mid-1940, the Mark I saw its first combat against the Italians late that year, a campaign in which the balance shifted with the arrival of Rommel and his Panzer IIIs, when the up-armored Crusader Mark II was brought quickly into service. This also proved inadequate against the Panzer IIIs and IVs, and the German 88 mm AA guns obliterated them.

Something needed to be done. While the Mark Is and IIs were put on screening and scouting duty, and the M3 Grants and M4 Shermans were put on the front line, it was obvious a new Crusader was needed as even in their secondary role, they suffered unacceptably high losses. In early 1942, the reliable 6 pdr gun was put in a redesigned and strengthened turret, the crew was reduced from five to three, and the commander acted as loader. While this overburdened him, like in some of the tanks early in the war, it also made for a more powerful model. By the time the Mark III Crusader was introduced, however, it was already being eclipsed by the better-designed Cromwell, the most popular of a new generation of heavy Cruiser tanks. About 5,300 Crusaders were built in total. While they never performed as well as the British had hoped, they did play their part in the early phases of the North African campaign.

The Mark VIII Cromwell was the culmination of Cruiser tank design. Faster than the Sherman and with a lower profile, it struck a good balance between firepower, speed, and armor. A total of 3,066 units were built, but many were used for training, though a limited number did see combat. The Cromwell measured 6.35 x 2.9 x 2.49 m (20.1 x 9.6 x 8.2 ft) and weighed 30.9 tons. It had a top speed of 64 km/h (40 mph) and a range of 270 km (170 mi). Its armor ranged from 15 to 76 mm (0.5 to 6 in). The four-man crew (commander, driver, gunner, and loader), served a 75 mm (2.95 in) main gun and two .303 (7.9 mm) machine guns.

Though it weighed more than other Cruiser Tanks, it had a powerful engine modified from the one used in the famous Spitfire fighter plane. Not only was this engine powerful but it was also light—the perfect combination for a more heavily-armored tank in which speed was a priority.

The Cromwell did not see active service until early 1944, by which time it had to face some of the toughest tanks the Third Reich ever designed. Cromwells participated in Operation Overlord, but the hedgerow country of Normandy was not suited to a tank relying on speed, and it fared poorly against the Panzers and Tigers. In one grim fight on June 13, 1944, a whole column of Cromwells was ambushed by a few Tigers, and all were nearly destroyed in less than 15 minutes. The model did much better once the Allies had broken through to more open terrain, but even then, crews found the new engine required much more maintenance than the sturdy American Sherman Tank.

A Cromwell tank in 1944

From 1942-1945, the British and Commonwealth nations relied on a large number of American Shermans, which proved their worth in North Africa and France. The British had even created their own modified form, an up-gunned Sherman, called the Firefly, with a 17-pounder (76.2 mm/3 in), high velocity main gun much more effective at taking out heavy German armor than the Sherman's standard issue 75 mm (2.95 in), with its low muzzle velocity.

The war in Europe and North Africa changed markedly with the arrival of the Americans in increasing numbers in 1942. A huge industrial base and large population made the United States a major force, but the Americans had fallen behind on tank design and lost many years in the Interwar period when the armored branch was underfunded and suffered from a lack of innovation. Like the French, the Americans did not have separate armored units and used the tanks for infantry support instead. The quick defeat of the French army prompted a rethink, and the government created a distinct armored service. When the war began, American military planners relied on the nation's incredible industrial resources to mass produce an astounding number of tanks, but their lack of research and development showed.

The first American tank to see action, the M3 Lee/Grant, was very much an interwar model. When war broke out in 1939, the U.S. lagged well behind in tank technology and production, and the M3 was the hasty, stopgap model. It had a 37 mm (1.46 in) gun on a small turret and a 75 mm (2.95 in) main gun on a sponson on the right side. This was because American engineers had yet to figure out how to put such a large gun in a turret. The sponson, a relic of World War I tanks like the British Mark IV, had a limited traverse and often required the driver to turn the whole tank so it could come into play, which cost precious seconds that could prove fatal. Early models had an upper cupola on the turret, housing a cal. 30 (7.62 mm) machine gun. One to three more machine guns were placed in the turret or the hull, although this varied widely between different production series.

There were two variations, with the Grant being shipped to the British and the Lee kept for domestic use. The M3 measured 5.95 x 2.61 x 3.1m (19.5 x 8.56 x 10.2 ft) and weighed 30 tons. The Lee had a seven member crew, while the Grant had six. It had a top speed of 42 km/h (26 mph) and a range of 195 km (121 mi). Armor ranged from 30-51 mm (1.18-2 in).

An M3 Grant on the left and M3 Lee on the right

The M3 saw action in the British army fighting in North Africa, starting in 1941 as a part of the Lend-Lease Act. There, they performed well against the Italian and German light tanks but not as well against the Panzer IIIs and IVs. Its unusually high profile made it an easy target, and the riveted hull proved brittle, but it had a durable design that gave a reliable performance in rough, desert conditions. Once the M4 Sherman became available, most surviving M3s were shipped to India and Burma. In the latter theater, they outmatched many Japanese tanks, although they fared badly against the heavier models. The Soviets also found they worked well in the dusty, snowy Russian steppe, but their innovations soon left the M3 behind.

A total of 6,258 units had been built, with the British getting 2,855 of them and the Soviets receiving 1,396.

The Americans also fielded a light tank early in the war, also designated the M3, but better known as the Stuart. It measured 4.33 x 2.23 x 2.35 m (14.21 x 7.32 x 7.71 ft) and weighed 14.7 tons. Its crew of four manned a 37 mm (1.45 in) main gun and three cal.30 (7.62 mm) machine guns, one coaxial with the main gun and another on top of the turret with another on the hull. Early models had an additional two machine guns in sponsons on either side of the turret, which were later disposed of to reduce the weight and leave more room inside the turret. The M3 Stuart had a top speed of 58 km/h (36 mph) and a range of 120 km (75 mi). Armor ranged from 13 to 51 mm (0.52-2 in) thick.

The tank was part of the Lend-Lease Program to the United Kingdom and Commonwealth nations (several thousand units) and the Soviets (just under 1,000 units), and this tank was also used by the Americans in their first major campaign, Operation Torch in North Africa in November of 1942. The Americans, British, and Free French invaded French Algeria in tandem with a big push from the east by the British that led to the Second Battle of El Alamein. The Stuart made quick work of the Italian tanks but proved highly vulnerable to the Panzer IIIs and IVs, as well as German artillery, as it had too many flat surfaces and the hull was riveted. A later version, the M5 introduced in 1942, had armor that was more sloped, but it was still no match for the Panzers.

A disabled M3 Stuart in North Africa

The improved version remained underpowered, especially considering what other countries had come out with in 1942, and the Soviets rejected an offer of them. In the European theater, both the M3 and M5 were consigned to screening and scouting roles. Most were sent to the Pacific theater where they did not have to face powerful tanks. Despite the M3's shortcomings, some 13,800 were built and served throughout the war. Almost 9,000 M5s were produced, many of them shipping to other nations as a part of Lend-Lease.

The main tank of the American war effort was the M4 medium tank, popularly known as the Sherman. This model was hastily introduced in 1941 after it quickly became clear that American tanks of the Interwar period would not hold up against the Panzers. It measured 5.84 x 2.62 x 2.74 m (19.16 x 8.6 x 8.99 ft), weighed 30.3 tons, and had a maximum speed of 48 km/h (30 mph) and a range of 193 km (120 mi). It had a crew of five: a commander, driver, co-driver, gunner, and loader. The turret was roomy enough to house the gunner and loader, and the commander sat just behind the loader. It had a 76 mm (3 in) armor on the front, 50 mm (1.97 in) on the sides, and 12.7 mm (0.5 in) on the top and bottom. In later models, the turret and upper hull were cast adding some strength, but it lagged well behind the German and Soviet tanks of its day. Later versions had increasingly thick armor but never really caught up with the opposition. Their high profile didn't help either. Like all tanks from this era, each unit came with a radio, a lesson the Allies quickly learned after the first disastrous year of the war. The crew had a good view—each of them was provided with a periscope able to turn 360 degrees with limited vertical movement.

An M4 Sherman

Its initial armament was a 75 mm (2.95 in) main gun in the turret, but it had a low muzzle velocity and poor penetration against most Panzers. It also had two cal.30 (7.62 mm) machine guns, one on the hull and one coaxial with the main gun. Later models also had a top-mounted heavy cal.50 Browning 12.7 mm (.5 in) machine gun able to cut through brick walls and lighter-armored vehicles, although the machine gunner was dangerously exposed.

Nearly 50,000 units of this model were produced, second only to the famous T-34 in terms of production for World War II tanks.

During the Second Battle of El Alamein (October 23–November 11, 1942), the British army's Shermans and Churchills performed well against Rommel's undersupplied and understrength forces. As Rommel himself described the typical British attacks, "In contact engagements the heavily gunned British tanks approached to a range of between 2,000 and 2,700 yards and then opened concentrated fire on our anti-tank and anti-aircraft guns and tanks, which were unable to penetrate the British armor at that range. The enormous quantities of ammunition which the enemy tanks used—sometimes they fired over thirty rounds at one target—were constantly replenished by armored ammunition carriers. The British artillery fire was directed by observers who accompanied the attack in tanks."

El Alamein was the first major campaign in which the Western Allies scored a decisive victory. The Germans and Italians had suffered more than 37,000 casualties, nearly a third of their entire force. The British and Commonwealth forces lost 13,500, a much lower number and a considerably smaller percentage of their army. While many factors led to victory, including Rommel's lack of supplies, his smaller army, the cracking of the German code, and Allied air superiority, the new, heavier tanks the British had fielded proved a major factor in the ultimate outcome. Winston Churchill said of the campaign, "Before Alamein, we never had a victory. After Alamein, we never had a defeat." While this was not strictly true, in hindsight, the battle can be seen as a major turning point of the war.

The Sherman's thin armor was not as much of a liability against Rommel's inferior forces, lacking as they did an appreciable quantity of later-model Panzers. This would change during the fighting in France, where close encounters with Panzer IVs, Vs, and VIs showed just how vulnerable the Sherman could be.

The hedgerow country made the perfect cover for ambushes. German infantry equipped with the Panzerfaust took out countless Shermans, the shaped charge blasting through the armor and often out the other side. While the holes looked small, they hid the carnage within as the Panzerfaust would send a spray of spall through the inside of the tank, ripping the crew apart.

The Panzers also proved deadly against the Shermans. Even the up-armored Panzer IVs were more than their match. Often the Shermans would catch fire when hit and both sides began to call them "Ronsons" after the popular brand of American lighter that advertised it "always lights the first time."

Sherman tank crews, like those of other under-armored tanks, took to piling sandbags on the front and back to keep enemy projectiles from exploding on the armor. It was meager protection, but it helped morale. Others strapped on scrap metal, sections of tank tracks, and even logs to add to their protection.

The Americans struggled to break out of the hedgerow country to the more open ground beyond where they might stand a chance. The problem was breaking through the hedgerows themselves. They had learned that driving in columns down any of the narrow French lanes meant a quick death since all had Panzers and infantry lurking in the cover beside them. One early solution was to fit a bulldozer blade on the front of a Sherman to smash through the hedgerows. Called "tankdozers," they worked well at first, but the Germans quickly learned to concentrate fire on them since they knew that an assault was sure to come just behind them.

Once again, the GIs were at an impasse until a clever sergeant, Curtis Culin, designed what he called a "hedge cutter" out of scrap metal. This was a relatively light, saw-toothed device made from spare metal and welded to the front of a tank. The thousands of beach obstacles the Germans had placed on the Normandy coast were used for metal, and the hedge cutter worked remarkably well. In time, the idea was to fit all the Shermans with them so the Germans wouldn't know from where the main attack would come.

The design was a great help in breaking out of hedgerow country, and Culin was awarded the Order of Merit. The American and British tanks remained at a decided disadvantage, however. To cut through the hedgerow, the tank first went up the earthen bank on which it grew, exposing the thin underside of the tank. This, at the same time, put the main gun and machine guns at such an angle they were unable to get bearings on the enemy. Culin's invention made it possible to break through the hedgerows, but it didn't make it easy.

Once through to more open ground, American artillery and planes were able to wield their full force against the Germans, but they still had a long, bitter fight ahead of them as they crossed the border into Germany and the enemy fought with greater resolve. The Shermans continued to lose heavily, but the Allies were now gaining momentum.

While the Sherman never got over its weaknesses, it arrived in Europe in vast quantities and was a reliable, fast, and easy-to-handle vehicle that was cheap to make. Its powerful engine gave it a good power-to-weight ratio that meant it could climb slopes that were impassible to any of the heavier Panzers. If well maintained, it rarely broke down. It could generally go up to 4,000 km (2,500 miles) before needing any maintenance at all. General Patton boasted that, "In mechanical endurance and ease of maintenance, our tanks are infinitely superior to any other." In the latter days of the war, it greatly outnumbered the Panzers, which suffered from a deteriorating industrial base and breakdowns.

An improved Sherman introduced in December of 1943 had a 76 mm (2.99 in) main gun. While only slightly larger than the original gun, it had a more powerful charge and a much higher muzzle velocity. A total of 3,396 units were produced until the end of the war.

Like many popular tank models, the Sherman came in many variants, including one with a 105 mm (4.13 in) howitzer for infantry support and various flamethrower models that proved effective when rooting out stubborn Japanese resistance on the Pacific Islands. Bridge layer, minesweeper, rocket launcher, and amphibious variants all saw wide use, proving the versatility of the basic Sherman design.

The only true American heavy tank was the M26 Pershing. Low, wide, and heavily armed and armored, it looked more like one of the later-model Panzers than an American tank. Introduced into the European theater in February of 1945, just three months before the fall of the Third Reich, it was the equal of the Panther, able to stand up even to the Tiger.

A Pershing

It measured 8.64 x 3.51 x 2.78 m (28.35 x 11.52 x 9.12 ft) and weighed 46 tons. It had a maximum speed of 35 km/h (22 mph) and a range of 160 km (100 mi). The crew of five (commander, gunner, loader, driver, and assistant driver) manned a 90 mm (2.95 in) main gun, two cal.30 (7.62 mm) machine guns (coaxial and hull) and a top-mounted cal.50 (12.7 mm) machine gun. They were protected by a hefty 100 mm (3.94 in) of armor on the front, 75 mm (2.95 in) on the sides, and 76 mm (3 in) on the turret.

Only 2,212 of this model were produced; most didn't even get to the front before the end of the war. Some authors assert that only 20 M26s, divided between the 3rd and 9th Armored Divisions, ever saw combat in World War Two. Many fought in the Korean War, where they performed well against the North Korean T-34s.

While the M26's role was limited, it pointed the way to a new generation of American tanks for the Cold War.

Later German Models

The Tiger II, also known as the Königstiger ("King Tiger"), was a final, desperate bid to win the tank war. This behemoth measured 6.40 (10.28 with the gun) x 3.75 x 3.09 m (21ft [33.73 with gun] x 12.3 x 10.14), weighed 69.8 tons, could go up to 41.5 km/h (25.8 mph) with a range of 170 km (110 m). Its crew of five (commander, driver, gunner, loader, and radio operator/machine-gunner) served an 88 mm (3.46 in) main gun and two—or in some units three—7.92 mm (0.31 in) machine guns. One machine gun was coaxial with the main gun and the other located on the front of the hull. A third was sometimes mounted atop the turret to be used as an anti-aircraft defense. This became increasingly important as Allied dominance of the skies left German armor vulnerable to bombing, although tank-mounted machine guns were never particularly effective against dive bombers. The crew was protected by 25 to 180 mm (1-7.08 inches) of armor.

A pair of Tiger IIs during the war

General Eisenhower looking at an overturned Tiger II

Only the heavy IS-2 tank could theoretically hope to take out its frontal armor, but that Soviet model's gun suffered from a shorter range, and in the open terrain of the Eastern Front, that proved a major liability. In fact, Allied studies after the war found no examples of a Tiger II being taken out by having its front armor penetrated.

The Kingtiger was fitted with several extras, such as watertight seals for fording rivers, an automatic fire extinguisher, and an automatic loading device. Its gun was truly devastating, with highly accurate telescopic sights and armor-piercing rounds able to break through between 153 mm and 238 mm (6.0 to 9.4 in) of armor at 2,000 m (1.2 miles). Gunners typically hit about 40% of the time at this range.

Unlike earlier tank models, the Tiger II never had time to sort out its teething problems. The first prototypes only came out in late 1943, and it consumed vast amounts of gasoline at a time when the Third Reich was suffering chronic fuel shortages and had numerous mechanical issues stemming from the fact it used the same engine and transmission as the Panther but weighed 25 tons more. During the long retreats of 1944 and 1945, many units were lost due to breakdowns or having simply run out of gas. The Tiger II was also hugely expensive, at 3 times the cost of a Tiger I and 10 times the cost of a T-34/85.

While the Tiger II was a masterful weapon, it suffered from a late introduction date at a point where German industry was already being pummeled into submission by Allied bombing. Only 492 units were ever produced, with production continuing into March of 1945. As was the case with all late model Panzers, its production was severely slowed by the Allied destruction of German factories. It's fair to wonder what would have happened if the Germans had been able to fend off those destructive bombing raids.

On an individual basis, the Tiger and Tiger II proved to be a fantastic success, with each unit generally claiming 10 tanks before being knocked out, but many units took out far more. At the Battle of Kursk on July 7, 1943, one Tiger under the command of SS-Oberscharführer Franz Staudegger took on some 50 T-34s. In a drawn out fight, it destroyed 22 Russian tanks and forced the rest to withdraw, but the relatively small number of Tigers at Kursk was unable to tip the balance in favor of the Germans, and the battle was ultimately lost.

After Kursk, the German campaign in the east became an increasingly defensive one, and the Tigers were shuttled to bolster troubled spots in the line. This wore them down mechanically, as did the many miles of retreating the Germans were doing.

Tigers also performed well against British and American tanks in North Africa, Italy, and Normandy, and they performed notable service against the Anzio bridgehead. Along with a complement of Panthers, 45 Tigers smashed through the Allied front lines, dealing heavy damage on Allied tanks. Only naval fire was able to force them to withdraw; not even the Tiger was able to stand up to a battleship's main guns.

They caused havoc in Normandy as well, but the difficult terrain of the hedgerows reduced their advantage. There, the farmland had been divided into small parcels screened off from one another by ridges of dirt topped with thick screens of bushes and trees. Sometimes these hedgerows were double, creating a trench between them and the perfect protection and camouflage for anti-tank units. In one odd incident, an Irish tanker, named Lt. Gorman, driving a Sherman, was trundling through this maze when he suddenly came across a Tiger II. Undaunted, Lt. Gorman ordered full speed ahead, and before the German tankers were able to turn their gun to fire, it rammed the Tiger, disabling it more effectively than the Sherman's 75 mm gun ever could. Having achieved his objective, Lt. Gorman ordered a hasty retreat before the Tiger blew his tank apart.

The Shermans enjoyed faster speed and maneuverability, and like Lt. Gorman, many tank commanders took advantage of the Tiger's slow turret traverse speed. The Allied tankers also used the Normandy terrain to outflank and gang up on the Tigers, but they still lost an average of six tanks for every Tiger taken out. In more open areas, the ratio was far higher thanks to the Tiger's superior gun range and armor. It wasn't until the introduction of the Russian T-34/85, IS-2, and American up-gunned Shermans in the middle of 1944, that any Allied tank could hope to go one-on-one with a Tiger. Even so, the Tigers still emerged the victor more often than not, but what really defeated the Panthers and Tigers were the Allied numbers.

During the Battle of the Bulge, the Germans fielded more than 100 Tigers and 90 Tiger IIs. The Germans smashed through the surprised American lines, already low on fuel at zero-hour. The entire plan hinged on taking various American fuel depots according to a precise schedule—which are, of course, impossible on the field of battle, especially in the middle of winter—and pretty soon, the Tigers sputtered to a halt. Many had been through days of heavy fighting, only to be abandoned with barely a dent on them.

Despite the tactics used by Allied ground forces, the only truly reliable way the Allies had to take out the Tiger and Tiger II was bombing. With their dominance of the skies in late 1944 through 1945, an increasing amount of German armor was hit by heavy bombs and rocket fire while having little in the way of defense.

Later Soviet Models

By 1942, the Soviets were mass producing T-34s at an astonishing rate, but they were not content with that excellent tank design and came up with even more powerful models as a response to the introduction of the German Panther. The first was the T-34/85, a modified T-34 with an 85 mm (3.35 in) main gun. While the bulk of the tank remained unchanged, the turret had to be completely redesigned.

The resulting tank measured 8.15 x 3 x 2.6 m (26.74 x 9.84 x 8.53 ft) and weighed 30.2 tons. It had a maximum speed of 38 km/h (26 mph) and a range of 185 km (114 mi). The crew of four manned the main gun and two 7.62 mm (0.3 in) machine guns, one in the hull and one coaxial. Armor ranged from 30 to 80 mm (1.18-3.15 in), and the turret was cast for extra strength. The more spacious turret allowed for three crewmen to sit inside—the gunner, loader, and commander. Thus, unlike the T-34, the commander didn't have to double as the loader.

The T-34/85 had its baptism of fire in early 1944 and by the middle of that year, outnumbered the original T-34/76 model. Its stronger gun proved capable of knocking out Panzers and Tigers, and its improved optical sighting equipment meant it could score kills at up to 1200 m (3,940 ft).

The tank did have some disadvantages: an overtaxed suspension gave a rough ride which reduced accuracy, and the high profile and blocky turret offered a tempting target for German tank crews. Even so, this design proved highly successful, and 17,600 units of the initial 1944 model were produced. It continued in production after the war and saw service in many countries during the Cold War. Including later models and Cold War production, the Soviet industry produced some 55,000 T-34/85s. Some were still serving as late as 1988 during the Iran-Iraq War.

The IS-2 tank was an even more robust upgrade. The initials stood for "Joseph Stalin," and it proved to be as fearsome as its namesake. Designed as a heavy tank, the 1944 model measured

9.9 x 3.10 x 2.73 m (32.48 x 10.17 x 8.96 ft) and weighed 46 tons. It had a speed of 37 km/h (23 mph) and a range of 240 km (150 mi). The crew of four (commander, gunner, loader, and driver) manned a 122 mm (4.8 in) main gun, three 7.62 mm (0.3 in) machine guns, and a top-mounted 2.7 mm (0.5 in) machine gun designed mainly for anti-aircraft use, although by this late in the war, Soviet tanks had little to fear from the Luftwaffe. Armor ranged from 30 to 120 mm (1.18-4.72 in). The thickness and steep slope of the frontal armor meant it could withstand the feared German 88 mm gun at 1,000 meters.

Only 3,854 units of the IS-2 were built, starting in 1944. It was a tiny amount by Soviet standards, but it was the model for many later Soviet tanks, and it saw service into the early 1960s. Because of their limited numbers during World War Two, they were assigned to elite Guards Battalions who were called upon to deal with special problems such as strong points or a group of King Tigers.

Hannah Zelenko's picture of an IS-2 (left) and an IS-3 (right)

This behemoth was not without its problems. Its gun was slow to reload, and it had a heavy, two-part shell, that even a good crew could only two or three rounds a minute. By contrast, a Panther crew was able to fire six or seven rounds in the same amount of time. The shells were so large that only 27 rounds could be stored inside the tank, compared to 64 rounds in the Tiger and 35 rounds in the T-34/85. Trucks would tag along behind the IS-2s carrying extra rounds, but they had to stay back during the fight or face destruction.

When famed German General Heinz Guderian examined a knocked out IS-2, he told his subordinates, "Do not get involved in a fight with a Stalin without overwhelming numerical superiority in the field. I believe that for every Stalin we must account for an entire platoon of Tigers. Any attempts by a single Tiger to fight a Stalin one-on-one can only result in the loss of a priceless war machine."

Both the T-34/85 and the IS-2 managed to take out a fair number Tigers on the Eastern Front, especially in cases where they ambushed the Tigers and were able to land hits at close range. The Germans, however, became adept at flanking these models and hitting them at close range in the sides or rear.

Tanks in Other Theaters

Though most of the discussion regarding World War II tanks focuses on North Africa and Europe, armored vehicles also fought in mainland Asia and the Pacific, and they were deployed by the Japanese and Allies.

Despite their impressive industrial capacity, the Japanese lagged behind the other great powers in tank development. Some tanks were used in their invasion of China in 1937, such as the Type 89 I-Go, the first Japanese medium tank to be built in large numbers starting in 1928. Based on the British Vickers Type C medium tank, about 400 were produced, and these were the backbone of Japanese armor during the Chinese invasion. The vehicle measured 5.73 x 2.13 x 2.56 m (18.79 x 7 x 8.4 ft) and weighed 10.9 tons with a pitiful speed of 16 km/h (10 mph) and a range of 150 km (95 mi). Its crew of four (commander, driver, gunner, and loader) was protected by a thin 6-17 mm (0.24-0.67 in), made weaker by the fact that it had been riveted. They served a 57 mm (2.24 in) gun and two 6.5 mm (.26 in) machine guns. The main gun was powerful enough to pierce 20 mm (0.79 in) of armor at 500 m (1,640 ft), although in the Chinese campaign, it was mostly used against pillboxes and other fortifications. The machine guns were placed at the front of the hull and, oddly, at the rear of the turret.

A picture of the tanks in 1942

The Japanese also fielded a large number of tankettes which, while out of date, proved capable against the Chinese who had few tanks and virtually no anti-tank weapons until later in the war. By 1939, the Type 89 and tankettes were outdated, and both were vulnerable to the T-26 and BT tanks. They were soon consigned to garrison and guard roles.

At the time of the invasion, the Chinese had been through years of factional warfare, and the various sides deployed a hodgepodge of outdated tanks, mostly imports such as the Renault FT and the Panzer I, plus a few more robust models such as the T-26. Overall, the Chinese armies had insufficient numbers of tanks and armored cars and as was the case with every other branch of service, found themselves outgunned by the invaders. Japanese tanks performed well against Chinese forces, but the vast distances and harsh conditions of the campaign put many out of service.

Japanese tanks also saw use in campaigns such as in the Philippines and Burma, where the thick jungle and numerous swamps made them quite ineffective. They fought on several Pacific islands against the Americans, but once again, the terrain was ill-suited for tank warfare, which discouraged the Japanese high-command from funding much in the way of tank development.

The main Japanese light tank during World War II was the Type 95 Ha-Go. It measured 4.38 x 2.06 x 2.18 m (14.37 x 6.76 x 7.15 ft), weighed 7.4 tons, had a top speed of 45 km/h (28 mph), and an impressive range of 250 km (400 mi). Its crew of three (driver, commander/gunner, and machine gunner) were protected by 6 to 16 mm (0.24-0.63 in) of armor and manned a 37 mm (1.46 in) main gun supplied with anti-tank rounds able to pierce 25 mm (0.98 in) of armor at 500 m (1,640 ft), plus two 7.7 mm (0.3 in) machine guns. One machine gun was fitted to the front of the hull, and the other angled on the right rear of the turret. This tank was meant as a faster option than the Type 89 that could be used not only for infantry support but for the type of motorized offensives that were becoming commonplace in European military theory.

The Type 95 suffered from thin armor and bad suspension, which made it difficult to fire without stopping first. Nevertheless, it saw use throughout the war, first doing well against the American M3 Stuarts in the Philippines in December 1941 but faring badly against later model American tanks. Some 2,300 of this model were built, the first rolling off the line in 1936.

The main Japanese medium tank of World War II was the Type 97 Chi-Ha, of which more than 2,000 were produced, starting in 1938. They measured 5.5 x 2.34 x 2.33 m (18 x 7.6 x 7.5 ft), weighed 15 tons, had a speed of 38 km/h (24 mph), and a range of 210 km (165 miles). Its crew of four (driver, machine gunner, commander/gunner, and secondary machine gunner/loader/radio operator) were protected by 8-25 mm (0.31-0.47 in) of armor. The main gun was a 57 mm (2.24 in) model, and it had two 7.7 mm (0.3 in) machine guns located on the front hull and rear turret.

A Type 97 Chi-Ha

The main gun had a low muzzle velocity and poor armor penetration capabilities, having been originally designed as an infantry support field gun. This gun proved useless against Russian armor and was replaced with a high velocity 47 mm (1.85 in) gun. It was a much better fit and helped win the Battle of Corregidor in the Philippines in 1942 by defeating the light American M3s. The Type 97 was ruggedly built and able to pass through thick jungle with apparent ease, often surprising the British and Americans who thought the terrain made them safe from armor.

Because of the relatively small number of tanks in the Japanese military, they never operated as separate units but almost always as infantry support.

In the island battles across the Pacific, the Japanese were faced with an overwhelming number of American tanks, and the Japanese infantry proved highly inventive in their anti-tank tactics, deploying a variety of anti-tank guns and bombs to knock out American armor. The thick jungle terrain of many of the Pacific islands helped. At times, groups of Japanese infantry would swarm onto a tank, set off bombs, and douse it with gasoline. American tank crews took to removing the top-mounted machine guns from their vehicles because brave Japanese soldiers would frequently leap onto the turrets and train the machine guns on the American infantry. In most cases, the man was promptly killed, but not before he'd inflicted serious losses on the Americans.

Anti-Tank Weapons

Perhaps not surprisingly, World War II witnessed the first mass production and innovation in anti-tank weapons. Wielded by infantry who could hide or sneak around to a tank's flanks or rear, they proved a major problem to tankers of all armies.

Anti-tank weapons came in two major types: field guns and handheld weapons. Field guns had already been used in the First World War to take out tanks, and in the Second World War they were designed for the purpose by making them more powerful, more mobile, and with a higher rate of fire.

The anti-tank rifle was another innovation. Used by the infantry ever since the final months of World War I, these oversized rifles came in a variety of models and ranged from 7.92 to 20 mm. What they had in common was an armor-piercing round that proved deadly to the light armor of the Interwar period, able to punch through about 13 mm (.51 in) at 275 meters (900 ft). They were the most numerous handheld anti-tank weapon at the beginning of the war. While they were effective against tanks such as the Panzer I or FT-17, the next generation of up-armored tanks made them far less useful. They were also heavy, sometimes more than a hundred pounds, and their long barrels made them awkward to handle. By 1942, they were a rare sight on the battlefield except with the Soviets, who continued to develop the weapon to make it more effective. In reality, however, it was never a reliable tank-killer, and the Soviets relied more on their artillery and tanks to take care of the Panzers.

Rocket-propelled grenades also became popular. The most famous was the German Panzerfaust, a cheap and efficient weapon firing a shaped charge able to puncture thick armor. Developed in 1943, this single-shot weapon fired a shaped charge from a tube. It was recoilless and could be fired by a single person. It was one of the first truly effective RPGs (Rocket Propelled Grenades), a weapon still being used today. The Panzerfaust was cheap to produce, easy to use, and effective. The most powerful mass-produced model, the Panzerfaust 100, could penetrate up to 200 millimeters (7.87 in) of armor. It tended to blow a small hole and tear the insides out of the tank armor, sending a large amount of spall ripping through the cabin.

A Panzerfaust

It did, however, have its drawbacks. The backblast meant it couldn't be fired from inside a bunker or building, and it also signaled to the target where the shooter was. It also had poor accuracy and an effective range of only 500 feet, and many of the conscripts using it were poorly trained and had to get much closer. In the last year of the war, it became the main weapon of the German *Volkssturm*, a hastily assembled militia of every able-bodied man (and some women) between 16 and 60.

Even in the hands of these raw recruits, the Panzerfaust proved to be a deadly weapon, and Allied tanks took care to always have infantry support on hand to clear the way. The Panzerfaust was especially dangerous in urban warfare, where the Germans might pop around a corner or from behind a pile of rubble and take out even the strongest of tanks.

An even more powerful model was the Panzerschreck. Based on the American bazooka, this 88 mm rocket launcher fired an armor-piercing projectile with an effective range of 150 m (492 ft) and was able to punch through up to 160 mm of armor.

The Panzerschreck was first produced in mid-1943, and though it proved effective, its short range and the large amount of smoke it produced made it dangerous to use. German troops jokingly called it the *Ofenrohr* ("Stove Pipe"). The launcher and its rockets were so bulky and heavy, they needed a two-man crew, unlike the lighter and easier to use Panzerfausts. German anti-tank units on the defensive would have a number of Panzerfausts and Panzerschrecks in staggered positions in trenches or in ruins at the wait until the enemy armor was well within effective range and then hit the tanks from various angles, ideally from the sides or rear.

A Panzerschreck

The American bazooka was less effective than these two weapons, but of an important design. Officially called the Rocket Launcher, M1A1, it was introduced in late 1942, in time for the nation's first major offensive in North Africa. Its simple design consisted of a metal tube into which the crew inserted a 60 mm (2.36 in) rocket grenade. In 1944, the improved M9 came out, followed by the M9A1. In all models, a battery ignited the rocket which, in the M9A1, was theoretically accurate up to about 274 meters (300 yards) and could pierce 127 mm (5 in) of armor. In reality, a bazooka was used at a third of that range to ensure the projectile hit a precise weak spot. Like the Panzerfaust and Panzerschreck, it had a large and visible backblast, announcing the position of the shooter to the entire battlefield. Its short range was not for the faint of heart. Unlike the Panzerfaust, it also required two men: a shooter and a loader.

An M1 Bazooka

Despite the dangers inherent in using a bazooka, it proved highly popular. Nearly half a million were made, many of which were sent via the Lend-Lease Program to the British, Free French, and Soviet Union, although the latter preferred their powerful anti-tank rifles which they favored until the end of the war. In addition to being a tank-killer, they proved effective against bunkers and buildings.

All three of these weapons were used to target weak points on an enemy tank - one simply did not point the device and fire. The rear and the engine compartment were favored targets as well as the tracks and wheels. Sometimes, the tougher tanks would require multiple shots.

Infantry facing a tank had to be clever, brave, and use the tank's weaknesses to their advantage. Many tank models, such as the Panzer V, had poor side vision. That and the weaker armor on the flanks encouraged anti-tank crews to come at it from the sides. Well-armed and determined infantry always posed a threat to a tank because individual men could hide and spread out to come at isolated tanks from all angles. Thus, tanks tried not to go anywhere without other armored vehicles and some infantry as backup.

All armies used passive anti-tank measures such as minefields, wide trenches, and physical barriers of metal or concrete to block off choke points and leave stationary tanks vulnerable to fire. A good example of this sort of passive protection occurred during the Second Battle of El Alamein. Rommel had dug in less than 100 km (60 mi) west of Alexandria, threatening British shipping. His ultimate goal was to take the port and move on to cut off the Suez Canal, but at the moment, he was too overstretched and undersupplied to continue the offensive. Instead, he went on the defensive, laying an extensive minefield in front of his position.

British Field Marshal Bernard Montgomery planned to break through these defenses and push the Germans and Italians back in tandem with the launching of Operation Torch, an Allied landing in French Algeria. The ultimate goal was to crush the Afrika Korps between these two forces, but first, he had to get through those minefields.

The battle started on the night of October 23 with Operation Lightfoot. After a heavy artillery preparation, the British infantry set out across the minefield under the cover of darkness to take the leading German positions and clear a way for the tanks along two corridors. Montgomery had named the operation "Lightfoot" because the infantry wouldn't set off the anti-tank mines if they stepped on them.

While all of this was supposed to have taken place in the first few hours, it ended up taking two days. At first, the mine-clearing went well, but when the tanks started to move through the relatively narrow corridor, the dust kicked up from the lead tanks obscured visibility to such an extent that a massive traffic jam ensued. In normal desert travel, vehicles spread out to avoid the dust of those in front of them, but there, that wasn't possible. Germans targeted the tank column and the advance ground to a halt. More than 50 British tanks were destroyed or disabled. Clearing the mines under fire was slow and deadly work, so the British tried to screen their activities with smoke, which only caused further confusion. In his report, Rommel's admiration for the British during Operation Lightfoot was made clear: "Particular skill was shown in carrying out this maneuver at night, and a great deal of hard training must have been done before the offensive."

The End of the War

As the noose tightened around the Third Reich in late 1944, German industry desperately tried to continue tank production. This was hampered by heavy Allied bombardment and a severe shortage of raw materials. Many older models of tanks, especially those captured in the early days of the war and relegated to police duties and training, found their way to the front; they did poorly. They had been put in the rear because they were out of date at the time, and after long years of development, they couldn't hope to survive.

Even with all the bombing and shortages, German industry worked wonders. An incredible 380 Panzer Vs were produced in March 1945, a little over a month before the fall of Berlin. One odd result of the bombing was an excess of Panzer V turrets—the factory that had produced them wasn't as badly damaged by bombing as the one producing the hulls, and the Germans were left with hundreds of turrets and nothing on which to mount them. A great many Panzer Vs were installed in concrete bases to be used as pillboxes in the final months of the war. Spare parts for all tanks also became a problem, with crews cannibalizing damaged tanks that might otherwise have been repaired and put back into service.

What German industry could not remedy was the chronic lack of fuel and raw materials. A shortage of manganese, essential for strengthening steel, meant the late war tank armor was not up to standard. Tanks broke down for lack of spare parts, lubricant, and gas. One British veteran recalled that he knew the end of the war was near when he saw long columns of undamaged German vehicles abandoned by the side of the road, their fuel tanks empty.

Even in the last weeks of the war, the Panthers and Tigers still caused mayhem in the Allied ranks. During the fighting around Berlin, a few surviving Tigers held key positions such as bridges, while most of the rest of the German armor was a useless dredging up of whatever tanks could be found in reserve and training units. Many of these had been captured in the first year or two of the war and hadn't seen service since. In an ultimate act of desperation, an old British Mark IV tank, captured in World War One and on display in a Berlin Museum, was dragged outside and used as a pillbox!

Facing the defenders of the German capital was a vast array of Soviet armor, including a large number of IS-2s. Firing high explosive rounds, they could collapse entire buildings, taking out the infantrymen defending them. The IS-2s were accompanied by infantry units, sappers, and flamethrower units to defend against Germans wielding Panzerfausts, but at least 67 had been knocked out by this fearsome tank-killer. Even in its death throes, the Wehrmacht and its tanks remained a deadly enemy.

Conclusion

As a thorough history of World War II indicates, the general perception that the Germans had the best tanks throughout the war is more myth than fact. In the opening battles, the French had better heavy tanks but a far inferior command and control system. The Panzers won because tank commanders had been given greater freedom of action and were able to quickly communicate with each unit as each tank came equipped with a radio. Also, the integration of every branch of service meant the Panzers could rely on the infantry, artillery, and Luftwaffe for support. More advanced tactics meant they could bring this concerted effort to bear on the weakest point of the Allied line and smash it.

In North Africa and the Eastern Front, German tactics continued to be superior to those of the Allies, even as they were outgunned by the improved Allied tanks. This was especially true on the Eastern Front, where the T-34 and later models proved superior to anything but the Tiger. Even when Soviet industry outmatched and outproduced German industry, the Red Army still took much higher losses than their German foes, thanks to better German tactics.

In the end, the Germans lost the tank war because they were vastly outnumbered by superior tanks at a time when the Third Reich suffered from shortages of raw materials and fuel. That they held out for so long is a testament to their fighting qualities and innovation.

Online Resources

Other World War II titles by Charles River Editors

Other titles about tanks on Amazon

Bibliography

Forczyk, Robert. *Erich Von Manstein*. Oxford, United Kingdom: Osprey Publishing, 2010.

Gunsburg, Jeffrey A. "The Battle of the Belgian Plain 12-14 May 1940: The First Great Tank Battle", in *The Journal of Military History*, Vol. 56, No. 2 (Apr., 1992), pp. 207-244.

Kaplan, Philip. *Rolling Thunder: A Century of Tank Warfare*. Barnsley, South Yorkshire, United Kingdom: Pen & Sword Books Ltd., 2013.

McLachlan, Sean and Charles River Editors. *The Tanks of World War I: The History and Legacy of Tank Warfare during the Great War*. Charles River Editors, 2017.

Porch, Douglas. "Military 'Culture' and the Fall of France in 1940" in *International Security*, Vol. 24, No. 4 (Spring, 2000), pp. 157-180.

Rottman, Gordon L. *World War II Anti-Tank Tactics*. Oxford, United Kingdom: Osprey Publishing, 2005.

Shepperd, Alan. *France 1940: Blitzkrieg in the West*. Oxford, United Kingdom: Osprey Publishing, 1990.

Sullivan, Brian R. "Fascist Italy's Military Involvement in the Spanish Civil War" in *The Journal of Military History*, Vol. 59, No. 4 (Oct., 1995), pp. 697-727.

Temperley, A. C. "Military Lessons of the Spanish War", in *Foreign Affairs*, Vol. 16, No. 1 (Oct., 1937), pp. 34-43.

Zaloga, Stephen J. *Poland 1939: The Birth of Blitzkrieg*. Oxford, United Kingdom: Osprey Publishing, 2002.

Free Books by Charles River Editors

We have brand new titles available for free most days of the week. To see which of our titles are currently free, click on this link.

Discounted Books by Charles River Editors

We have titles at a discount price of just 99 cents everyday. To see which of our titles are currently 99 cents, click on this link.

Made in the USA
Middletown, DE
28 September 2021